W9-DCZ-199

HORIZON

SEPTEMBER, 1960 · VOLUME III, NUMBER 1

SOIT · QVI MAL Y PENSE

HORIZON

A Magazine of the Arts

SEPTEMBER, 1960 *VOLUME III, NUMBER 1*

HORIZON is published every two months by American Horizon, Inc., a subsidiary of American Heritage Publishing Co., Inc., 551 Fifth Avenue, New York 17, N. Y.
Single Copies: $3.95
Annual Subscriptions: $18.00 in the U.S. & Can.
$19.00 elsewhere

Second-Class postage paid at New York, N.Y.

COVER: Napoleon Bonaparte, first consul of France, points the way south and across the Alps at the head of forty thousand troops about to cross the Great Saint Bernard pass to descend upon the Austrian army. "I would be painted calm and serene on a fiery steed" were his instructions to his court painter, Jacques Louis David, for this portrait done after the ensuing victory at Marengo in June, 1800, and now in a private French collection. By loot and treaty, Napoleon's forces gained many of Italy's greatest paintings and sculpture for the new museum wings of the Louvre in Paris. For a history of the Louvre and Napoleon's part in it, see page 57.

FRONTISPIECE: From the thirteenth to the sixteenth century, Englishmen often memorialized their dead by carving almost life-sized effigies of them on brass plates and inserting these into the floor of the local church. Because they are decorative and depict authentic costume, rubbings have long been made of the best preserved of the some 10,000 brasses extant. Recently an exhibition of the rubbings, mounted as wall hangings, was held in St. James's Church in New York. One of the handsomest was this one made from plates laid down in Hever, Kent, in 1538 to commemorate Sir Thomas Boleyn, father of the ill-fated Anne.

At the close of Ingmar Bergman's *The Seventh Seal* (1957) occurs the macabre dance scene below, in which Death leads off the key figure in the film—a knight returned from the Crusades—and others in his party. Spared is a visionary strolling player together with his family, and he exclaims to his wife:

I see them, Mia! Over there against the dark stormy sky. They are all there—the smith and Lisa and the knight and Raval and Jöns and Skat. And Death, the severe master, invites them to dance. He tells them to hold each other's hands, and they tread the dance in a long row. And first goes the master with his scythe and hourglass, but Skat dangles at the end with his lyre. They dance away from the dawn and it's a solemn dance towards the dark lands, while the rain washes their faces, cleans the salt of the tears from their cheeks. . . .

"A film for me begins with something very vague— a chance remark . . . a few bars of music . . . a shaft of light across the street. . . ." So writes the most widely acclaimed film director of our time

Ingmar Bergman: Why I Make Movies

During the shooting of *The Virgin Spring,* we were up in the northern province of Dalarna in May and it was early one morning, about half past seven. The landscape there is rugged, and our company was working beside a little lake in the forest. It was very cold, about 30 degrees, and from time to time a few snowflakes fell through the gray, rain-dimmed sky. The company was dressed in a strange variety of clothing—raincoats, oil slickers, Icelandic sweaters, leather jackets, old blankets, coachmen's coats, medieval robes. Our men had laid some ninety feet of rusty, buckling rail over the difficult terrain, to dolly the camera on. We were all helping with the equipment—actors, electricians, make-up men, script girl, sound crew—mainly to keep warm. Suddenly someone shouted and pointed toward the sky. Then we saw a crane high above the fir trees, and then another, and then several cranes, floating majestically in a circle above us. We all dropped what we were doing and ran to the top of a nearby hill to see the cranes better. We stood there for a long time, until they turned westward and disappeared over the forest. And suddenly I thought: this is what it means to make a movie in Sweden.

PHOTOGRAPHS JANUS FILMS

At left, a couple in Bergman's *Smiles of a Summer Night* (1956) rouse themselves after a night in a haystack, and the script runs:

Now it is just before dawn. A light mist lies over the water. The morning breeze touches the birches, and birds begin to sing. Frid gets up from the haystack, takes a deep breath, and raises his arm in an expansive gesture.

Frid: *Now the summer night smiles its second smile: for the clowns, the fools, the unredeemable.*
Petra: *Then she smiles for us. . . .*
Frid: *Are you thirsty, do you want a beer?*
Petra: *I said that she smiles for us.*
Frid: *I agree. (He drinks.) Now she smiles for us.*
Petra: *Will you marry me?*
Frid: *Hahahahaha!*
Petra: *An hour ago you said that you wanted to. . . .*
Frid: *Hahahahaha! That was* then.

Petra looks up. Then she gives him a hard slap across the face, but he continues to laugh.

Petra: *You* shall *marry me.*
Frid: *Hahahahaha! You're a strong sugar plum.*

This is what can happen, this is how we work together with our old equipment and little money, and this is how we can suddenly drop everything for the love of four cranes floating above the treetops.

My association with film goes back to the world of childhood. My grandmother had a very large old apartment in Uppsala. I used to sit under the dining-room table there, "listening" to the sunshine that came in through the gigantic window. The bells of the cathedral went ding-dong, and the sunlight moved about and "sounded" in a special way. One day, when winter was giving way to spring and I was five years old, a piano was being played in the next apartment. It played waltzes, nothing but waltzes. On the wall hung a large picture of Venice. As the sunlight moved across the picture, the water in the canal began to flow, the pigeons flew up from the square, gesticulating people were engaged in inaudible conversation. Bells sounded, not from Uppsala Cathedral, but from the picture itself. And the piano music also came from that remarkable picture of Venice.

A child who is born and brought up in a vicarage acquires an early familiarity with life and death behind the scenes. Father performed funerals, marriages, baptisms; he gave advice and prepared sermons. The Devil was an early acquaintance, and in the child's mind there was a need to personify him. This is where my magic lantern came in. It consisted of a small metal box with a carbide lamp—I can still remember the smell of the hot metal—and colored glass slides: Red Riding Hood and the Wolf, and all the others. The Wolf was the Devil, without horns but with a tail and a red mouth, strangely real yet incomprehensible, a picture of wickedness and temptation on the flowered wall of the nursery.

When I was ten years old I received my first, rattling film projector, with its chimney and lamp. I found it both mystifying and fascinating. The first film I had was nine feet long and brown in color. It showed a girl, lying asleep in a meadow, who woke up and stretched out her arms, then disappeared to the right. That was all there was to it. The film was a great success and was projected every night until it broke and could not be mended any more.

This little rickety machine was my first conjuring set. And even today I remind myself with childish excitement that, since cinematography is based on deception of the human eye, I really am a conjurer. I have worked it out that if I see a film with a running-time of one hour, I sit through twenty-seven minutes of complete darkness—the blankness between frames. When I show a film, I am guilty of deceit. I use an apparatus which is constructed to take advantage of a certain human weakness, an apparatus with which I can sway my audience in a highly emotional manner—make them laugh, scream with fright, smile, believe in fairy stories, become indignant, feel shocked, charmed, deeply moved, or perhaps yawn with boredom. Thus I am either an impostor or, where the audience is willing to be taken in, a conjurer. I perform conjuring tricks with apparatus so expensive and so wonderful that any performer in history would have given anything to own or to make use of it.

A film for me begins with something very vague—a chance remark or a bit of conversation, a hazy but agreeable event unrelated to any particular situation. It can be a few bars of music, a shaft of light across the street. Sometimes in my work at the theater I have envisioned actors made up for yet unplayed roles.

These are split-second impressions that disappear as quickly as they come, yet leave behind a mood—like pleasant dreams. It is a mental state, not an actual story, but one abounding in fertile associations and images. Most of all, it is a brightly colored thread sticking out of the dark sack of the unconscious. If I begin to wind up this thread, and do so carefully, a complete film will emerge.

In Bergman's script for *The Magician,* a little scullery maid and an old crone of the magician's troupe whisper in a corner:

Grandmother: *Why do you cry, little ant?*
Sanna: *Are you a witch?*
Grandmother: *Perhaps.*
Sanna: *I'm so frightened of everything that's happened tonight. (Quietly.) And you are so old and ugly.*
Grandmother: *When you are almost two hundred years old, you'll be ugly, too, little ant. . . .*
Sanna: *Can you also perform magic?*
Grandmother: *It's happened. But nowadays, nobody believes in my secrets, so I have to be careful. One must not offend the new faith, because then one might be put into a madhouse. . . .*
Sanna: *How did you become a witch?*
Grandmother: *Shh! I can't tell you that.*
Sanna: *Have you sold your soul?*
Grandmother: *Yes. Perhaps I have.*
Sanna *(crying)*: *Oh! I'm becoming frightened again.*
Grandmother: *Now go along to bed, and the witch will give you a gift. Do what I say, little ant. I only want the best for you.*

This primitive nucleus strives to achieve definite form, moving in a way that may be lazy and half-asleep at first. Its stirring is accompanied by vibrations and rhythms that are very special, and unique to each film. The picture sequences then assume a pattern in accordance with these rhythms, obeying laws born out of and conditioned by my original stimulus.

If that embryonic substance seems to have enough strength to be made into a film, I decide to materialize it. Then comes something very complicated and difficult: the transformation of rhythms, moods, atmosphere, tensions, sequences, tones, and scents into words and sentences, into an understandable screenplay.

This is an almost impossible task.

The only thing that can be satisfactorily transferred from that original complex of rhythms and moods is the dialogue, and even dialogue is a sensitive substance which may offer resistance. Written dialogue is like a musical score, almost incomprehensible to the average person. Its interpretation demands a technical knack plus a certain kind of imagination and feeling—qualities which are often lacking even among actors. One can write dialogue, but how it should be delivered, its rhythm and tempo, what is to take place between the lines—all this must be omitted for practical reasons. A script with that much detail would be unreadable. I try to squeeze instructions as to location, characterization, and atmosphere into my screenplays in understandable terms, but the success of this depends on my writing ability and the perceptiveness of the reader, which are not predictable.

Now we come to essentials, by which I mean montage, rhythm, and the relation of one picture to another: the vital third dimension without which the film is merely a dead product from a factory. Here I cannot clearly give a key, as in a musical score, or a specific idea of the tempo which determines the relationship of the elements involved. It is quite impossible for me to indicate the way in which the film "breathes" and pulsates.

I have often wished for a kind of notation which would enable me to put on paper all the shades and tones of my vision, to record distinctly the inner structure of a film. For when I stand in the artistically devastating atmosphere of the studio, my hands and head full of all the trivial and irritating details that go with motion-picture production, it often takes a tremendous effort to remember how I originally saw and thought out this or that sequence, or what the relation was between the scene of four weeks ago and that of today. If I could express myself clearly, in explicit symbols, then the irrational factors in my work would be almost eliminated, and I could work with absolute confidence that whenever I liked I could prove the relationship between the part and the whole and put my finger on the rhythm, the continuity of the film.

Thus the script is a very imperfect *technical* basis for a film. And there is another important point which I should like to mention in this connection. Film has nothing to do with literature; the character and substance of the two art forms are usually in conflict. This probably has something to do with the receptive process of the mind. The written word is read and assimilated by a conscious act of the will in alliance with the intellect; little by little it affects the imagination and the emotions. The process is different with a motion picture. When we experience a film, we consciously prime ourselves for illusion: putting aside will and intellect, we make way for it in our imagination. The sequence of images plays directly on our feelings without touching on the intellect.

Music works in the same fashion; I would say that there is no art form that has as much in common with film as music. Both affect our emotions directly, not by way of the intellect. And film is mainly rhythm; it is inhalation and

A characteristic shot that appears in Bergman's latest movie, The Virgin Spring, *shows a father planting a tree over the spot where his daughter was ravished and then killed by three shepherds.*

exhalation in continuous sequence. Ever since childhood, music has been my greatest source of recreation and stimulation, and I often experience a film or play musically.

It is mainly because of this difference between film and literature that we should avoid making films out of books. The irrational dimension of a literary work, the germ of its existence, is often untranslatable into visual terms—and it, in turn, destroys the special, irrational dimension of the film. If, despite this, we wish to translate something literary into film terms, we must make an infinite number of complicated adjustments which often bear little or no fruit in proportion to the effort expended.

I myself have never had any ambition to be an author. I do not want to write novels, short stories, essays, biographies, or even plays for the theater. I only want to make films—films about conditions, tensions, pictures, rhythms, and characters that are in one way or another important to me. The motion picture and its complicated process of birth are my methods of saying what I want to my fellow men. I am a film maker, not an author.

Thus the writing of the script is a difficult period but a useful one, for it compels me to prove logically the validity of my ideas. In doing this, I am caught in a conflict—a conflict between my need to transmit a complicated situation through visual images and my desire for absolute clarity. I do not intend my work to be solely for the benefit of myself or the few but for the entertainment of the general public. The wishes of the public are imperative. But sometimes I risk following my own impulse, and it has been shown that the public can respond with surprising sensitivity to the most unconventional line of development.

When shooting begins, the most important thing is that those who work with me feel a definite contact, that all of us somehow cancel out our conflicts through working together. We must pull in one direction for the sake of the work at hand. Sometimes this leads to dispute, but the more definite and clear the "marching orders," the easier it is to reach the goal which has been set. This is the basis of my conduct as director, and perhaps the explanation for much of the nonsense that has been written about me.

While I cannot let myself be concerned with what people think and say about me personally, I believe that reviewers and critics have every right to interpret my films as they like. I refuse to interpret my work to others, and I cannot tell the critic what to think; each person has the right to understand a film as he sees it. Either he is attracted or repelled. A film is made to create reaction. If the audience does not react one way or another, it is an indifferent work and worthless.

I do not mean by this that I believe in being "different" at any price. A lot has been said about the value of originality, and I find it foolish; either you are original or you are not. It is completely natural for artists to take from and give to each other, to borrow from and experience one another. In my own life, my great literary experience was Strindberg. There are works of his which can still make my hair stand on end—*The People of Hemsö,* for example. And it is my dream to produce his *Dream Play* someday. Olof Molander's production of it in 1934 was for me a fundamental dramatic experience.

On a personal level, there are many people who have meant a great deal to me. My father and mother were certainly of vital importance, not only in themselves but because they created a world for me to revolt against. In my family there was an atmosphere of hearty wholesomeness which I, a sensitive young plant, scorned and rebelled against. But that strict middle-class home gave me a wall to pound on, something to sharpen myself against. At the same time my family taught me a number of values—efficiency, punctuality, a sense of financial responsibility—which may be "bourgeois" but are nevertheless important to the artist. They are part of the process of setting oneself severe standards. Today as a film maker I am conscientious, hard-working, and extremely careful; my films involve good craftsmanship, and my pride is the pride of a good craftsman.

Among the people who have meant something in my professional development is Torsten Hammaren of Göteborg. I came there from Hälsingborg, where I had been head of the municipal theater for two years. I had no conception of what theater was; Hammaren taught me during the four years I stayed in Göteborg. Then, when I wrote my first screenplay, *Torment,* Alf Sjöberg, who directed it, taught me a great deal, as did Lorens Marmstedt after I had directed my first (unsuccessful) movie. Among other things, I learned from Marmstedt the one unbreakable rule: you must look at your own work very coldly and clearly; you must be a devil to yourself in the screening room when watching the day's rushes. Then there is Herbert Grevenius, one of the few who believed in me as a writer. I had trouble with script writing and was reaching out more and more to the drama, to dialogue, as a means of expression. He gave me great encouragement.

Finally, there is Carl Anders Dymling, my producer. He is crazy enough to place more faith in the creative artist's sense of responsibility than in calculations of profit and loss. I am thus able to work with an integrity that has become the very air I breathe—one of the main reasons I do not want to work outside of Sweden. The moment I lose this freedom I will cease to be a film maker, because I have no skill in the art of compromise. My only significance in the world of film lies in the freedom of my creativity.

Today, the ambitious film maker is obliged to walk a tightrope without a net. He may be a conjurer, but no one conjures the producer, the bank director, or the theater owners when the public refuses to go to see a film and lay down the money by which producer, bank director, theater owner, and conjurer live. The conjurer may then be deprived of his magic wand. I would like to be able to measure the amount of talent, initiative, and creative ability that has been destroyed by the film industry in its ruthlessly efficient sausage-machine. What was play to me once has now become a struggle. Failure, criticism, public indifference all hurt more today than yesterday. The brutality of the industry is unmasked—yet that can be an advantage.

So much for people and the film business. I have been asked, as a clergyman's son, about the role of religion in my thinking and film making. To me, religious problems are continuously alive. I never cease to concern myself with them, and my concern goes on every hour of every day. Yet it does not take place on the emotional level but on an intellectual one. Religious emotion, religious sentimentality, is something I got rid of long ago—I hope. The religious problem is an intellectual one to me: the problem of my mind in relation to my intuition. The result is usually some kind of tower of Babel.

Philosophically, there is a book which was a tremendous experience for me: Eino Kaila's *Psychology of the Personality*. His thesis that man lives strictly according to his needs—negative and positive—was shattering to me, but terribly true. And I built on this ground.

People ask what are my intentions with my films—my aims. It is a difficult and dangerous question, and I usually give an evasive answer: I try to tell the truth about the human condition, the truth as I see it. This answer seems to satisfy everyone, but it is not quite correct. I prefer to describe what I would *like* my aim to be.

There is an old story of how the Cathedral of Chartres was struck by lightning and burned to the ground. Then thousands of people came from all points of the compass, like a giant procession of ants, and together they began to rebuild the cathedral on its old site. They worked until the building was completed—master builders, artists, laborers, clowns, noblemen, priests, burghers. But they all remained anonymous, and no one knows to this day who rebuilt the Cathedral of Chartres.

A Bergman touch in another mood is this nostalgic scene in Wild Strawberries *of a summer holiday among Swedish middle-class folk—the milieu from which Bergman himself sprang.*

Regardless of my own beliefs and my own doubts, which are unimportant in this connection, it is my opinion that art lost its basic creative drive the moment it was separated from worship. It severed an umbilical cord and now lives its own sterile life, generating and degenerating itself. In former days the artist remained unknown and his work was to the glory of God. He lived and died without being more or less important than other artisans; "eternal values," "immortality," and "masterpiece" were terms not applicable to his case. The ability to create was a gift. In such a world flourished invulnerable assurance and natural humility.

Today the individual has become the highest form, and the greatest bane, of artistic creation. The smallest wound or pain of the ego is examined under a microscope as if it were of eternal importance. The artist considers his isolation, his subjectivity, his individualism almost holy. Thus we finally gather in one large pen, where we stand and bleat about our loneliness without listening to each other and without realizing that we are smothering each other to death. The individualists stare into each other's eyes and yet deny each other's existence. We walk in circles, so limited by our own anxieties that we can no longer distinguish between true and false, between the gangster's whim and the purest ideal.

Thus if I am asked what I would *like* the general purpose of my films to be, I would reply that I want to be one of the artists in the cathedral on the great plain. I want to make a dragon's head, an angel, a devil—or perhaps a saint—out of stone. It does not matter which; it is the sense of satisfaction that counts. Regardless of whether I believe or not, whether I am a Christian or not, I would play my part in the collective building of the cathedral.

Ingmar Bergman will be represented in the United States this fall by a new film, The Virgin Spring, *and by a new book,* Four Screenplays of Ingmar Bergman *(Simon & Schuster), to which the foregoing article will serve as introduction.*

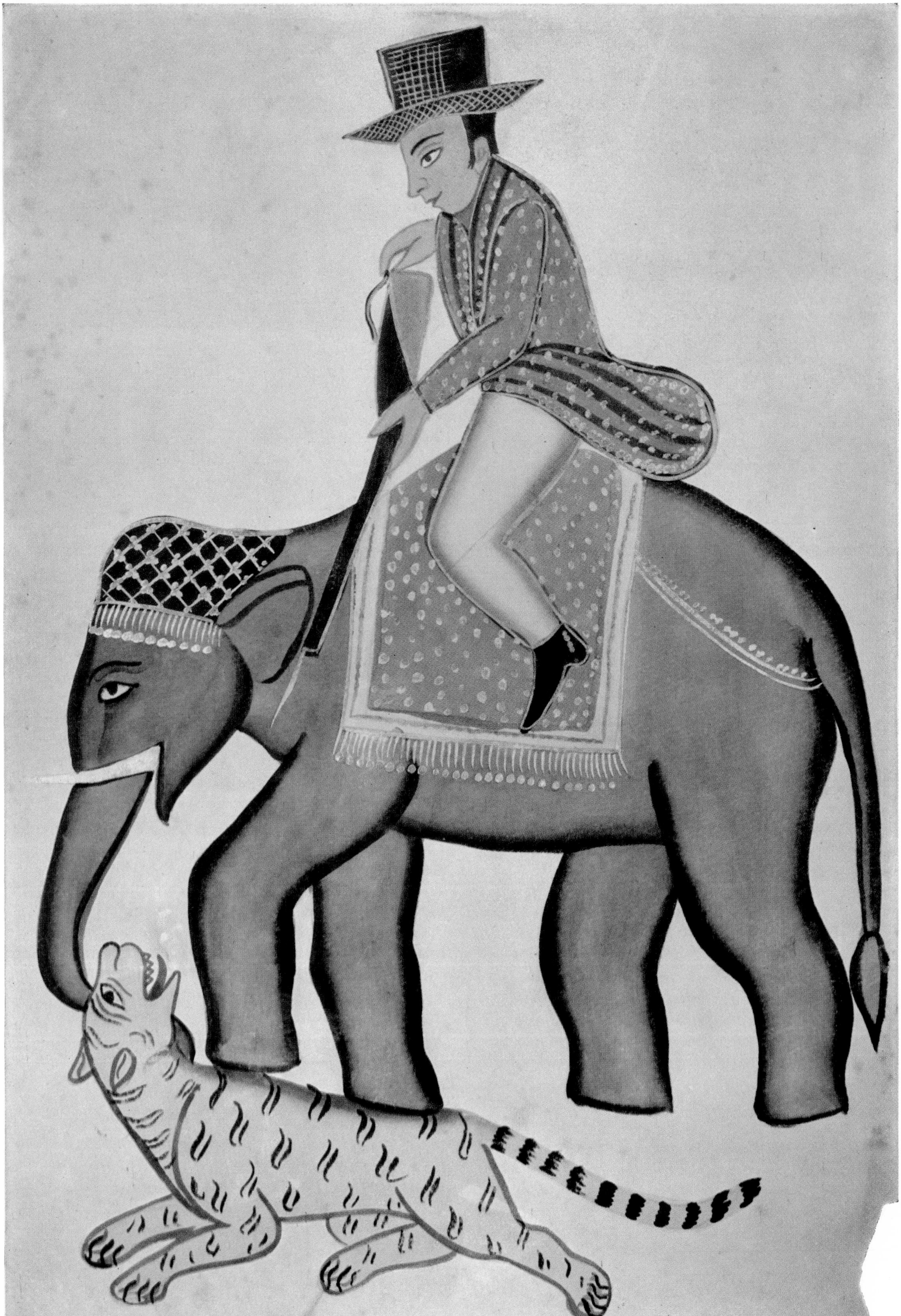

By ALAN MOOREHEAD

THE COMING OF THE WHITE MAN

To every distant shore, some time in the last five hundred years, the light-skinned stranger came, bearing Western civilization. His image, seen by native artists, was scratched on rock, carved in wood, woven in cloth, or painted on paper. Now, as the tide of white expansion ebbs, this graphic record remains to mark a fateful moment in the history of world culture

Captain James Cook, sailing up the unexplored southeastern coast of Australia in May, 1770, had a curious experience. When his ship, the *Endeavour,* anchored close to land in the vicinity of Botany Bay, the natives on shore took no notice whatever. An old woman and some children, all of them quite naked, appeared before a group of huts and, having made a fire, "set about dressing their dinner with perfect composure." There were some men about as well, and they, too, appeared to be very little alarmed or disturbed by this sudden, extraordinary visitation from the outside world.

The *Endeavour,* certainly, was not a very big ship—she was only 370 tons and carried a crew of 85—but she was the first glimpse of civilization these aborigines had ever had, and no doubt to a primitive mind she was beyond all comprehension: she was as strange and inexplicable as some sudden phenomenon of the natural elements, the piling-up of storm clouds in the sky, an eclipse of the sun, or perhaps, more simply, a giant uprooted tree that had floated up onto the coast. And since it is a basic human instinct to fear the unknown and, if possible, to disregard it—if you pretend not to see the monster, perhaps he won't notice you—the aborigines went on with their dinner.

Captain Cook ordered a longboat to the shore, and as it drew near, the natives saw that there were men on board: not men whom they could regard as normal in any way, since they had white faces and extraordinary coverings on their bodies, but still quite definitely men. Then, at last, the natives experienced the shock of recognition. This was something they could understand, and they reacted as, probably, we would react in similar circumstances: they prepared to defend themselves.

An Englishman on a tiger hunt was painted by an Indian artist of the Kalighat, or bazaar, school of the late nineteenth century. The habits and customs of the colonizers had by then become familiar to the natives of the land they ruled.

Captain Cook threw them some "beads, nails, and other trifles" and "used every possible means to convince them that no injury was intended." But it was all to no purpose: as soon as the crew began to disembark, the natives attacked them with spears and had to be driven off with a discharge of muskets.

Captain Cook was a laconic man, and we do not know all the details of the parleying that followed, but it seems that, in the end, the natives were won round. In a day or two they had grown accustomed to the white men's faces, and if the natives were not yet absolutely friendly, they were filled at least with a passive and overwhelming curiosity.

This first contact between whites and primitive colored men is a fascinating moment, and it seems to have followed roughly the same pattern wherever it occurred—whether it was Vasco da Gama landing in east Africa, Columbus in the West Indies, or Cook in Australia. Naturally the native was bewildered. The late Professor Julius E. Lips, author of *The Savage Hits Back,* was hardly exaggerating when he said, "The first appearance of the white man in tribal territory produced astonishing emotions—excitement such as we might feel if we were suddenly to meet, in Trafalgar Square or Times Square, beings who had descended from Mars." In countries like India, China, and Japan, where an advanced culture was already in existence when the first white men arrived, the shock was naturally less profound. But to the natives of Africa and the South Seas, the white man was an awesome and frightening spectacle. Often he was regarded as some kind of demigod, a tribal chieftain who had returned from the ghostly kingdom of the dead and who was now endowed with magical and supernatural powers.

Only a few years ago I myself had such an encounter. I was traveling with a friend on rather a foot-loose journey through southeast Asia, and we were about to fly down to Bali from Singapore when someone suggested that it would be a much more interesting experience to visit the Dyaks who were still living an isolated life in the jungles of northern Borneo.

It seemed at the time to be an excellent idea—every traveler likes to go places where he thinks no one else has been before—and we crossed over by sea to the British crown colony of Sarawak on the northern coast of Borneo. At Kuching, the tiny capital of the place, we found a guide-interpreter and, with a little string of porters carrying our bedding and stores, set off for the interior. I cannot pretend that during the next few weeks we penetrated into any really unexplored country, but we did at least meet tribesmen who rarely, if ever, had seen a white man before.

In particular I remember arriving one evening just before dark at a village which consisted simply of a single rickety wooden building (known in Borneo as a longhouse) built above the banks of a river with thick jungle all around. The women, with sarongs round their waists and bamboo buckets slung over their shoulders, had come down to the river to fetch water for the night when they heard us approaching through the trees above them on the opposite bank. They stood for a moment absolutely rigid, staring at us with the intensity of wild animals that have been suddenly surprised. Then, with one accord, they turned and bolted for the longhouse, chattering and screaming to one another as they ran. By the time we got down to the river and waded across it, we could see glimpses of their men hiding behind trees and bushes, watching our approach. We smiled, we waved, we used every possible means to convince them that no injury was intended, and by the time we got to the steps of the longhouse, they had gathered in a body around us.

There is a great tradition of hospitality among the Dyaks, and we were escorted onto the veranda of the building, offered food (rice in earthenware pots), and shown a place where we could spread out our bedding for the night. Presently children began to appear in the doorways along the veranda, and they were followed after a little time by the women. Within half an hour we were surrounded at a distance of two or three feet by a ring of staring faces. They stared and stared. They practically gobbled us up with their staring. One's slightest gesture—the lighting of a cigarette, a smile, the crossing of one's legs—was followed with an intense, burning curiosity, and each new article that was brought out of our porters' packs was greeted with an outburst of excited comment. These were not circumstances that called for excessive modesty, but even so it was a slight ordeal getting undressed with that wall of faces pressing around us. Every particle of one's shrinking white body was scrutinized and appraised with cries of astonishment. And so it continued through the hot, mosquito-ridden night. Whenever I woke, I saw by the light of the cooking fires that same ring of curious, staring eyes.

Now there was nothing really abnormal or unexpected about all this, yet by the time we came to leave on the following day, it was quite evident that an incident of some importance had occurred in these people's lives—as indeed it had in ours. For weeks to come we were going to be described and discussed in the village; every detail of our appearance and our clothing, the very sound of our voices was going to be recalled. This first impression of the men of the outside world was going to fix itself in tribal legend, just as, presumably, Captain Cook and his men fixed their images in the minds of the Australian aborigines.

We have, fortunately, a means of knowing something about these images. All over the world the coming of the white man has been recorded by native artists in the form of drawings and paintings, figurines carved in wood or ivory or modeled in clay, totem poles, and such artifacts as decorated drums and tribal weapons. Some of the results of this work are presented on these pages by John Maass. It is a collection which has a special interest at the present time since it is clear that we are coming to the end of an era. There are not now many places in the world where one can undergo an experience such as I have described above. The great outburst of white expansion round the globe that began in the fifteenth and sixteenth centuries is coming to an end at last. Nearly everywhere, contact between whites and colored peoples has already been made and even developed to a point of intimate familiarity. There have been, of course, many complications in this relationship, many breaks and setbacks. At the end of the last century, for instance, a wave of xenophobia swept over China, and the Boxer Uprising against the white man was a ruthless and bloody business while it lasted. The Indian Mutiny of 1857 is another landmark in the history of racial relations. Prior to it, the color bar was not a lively issue in India. Intermarriage between whites and Indians was fairly common, and illicit unions were legion. The British colonel in charge of a district would tend to know the local ruler and his family almost as well as he knew his own soldiers; he and his officers would engage in polo matches and hunting expeditions with the maharajah and his court, his wife would visit the maharanee, and the children of the two families would play together. But the hostilities of 1857 put a stop to these friendships, and a century has hardly sufficed to re-establish the old easygoing relationship between Europeans and Indians in local social life.

Such upheavals have continued, as everybody knows, to the present day, but it is a fairly safe assumption that despite these antagonisms, white and colored peoples are now drawing closer together, or at any rate they are meeting on terms of greater equality. Even within our own lifetimes, the most primitive Africans have learned to wear clothes, to read and write, to administer their own governments and adopt Western ways. It is no longer a great wonder that a Negro can be a surgeon, a sea captain, an actor, or a banker. The world is leveling out.

The importance of the drawings and illustrations on these pages is that most of them antedate the commotions of the last hundred years or so. They carry us directly back to the beginning of things and give us a glimpse of ourselves as we seemed to the fresh and curious eye of the native artist when our ancestors first intruded into his village.

It is not always a flattering image of the white man that the native artist produced, since he soon learned that the white man was something less than divine: the slaver and the trader followed in the wake of the explorer and the missionary. Yet it will be seen from these illustrations that it was a spontaneous and candid portrait that emerged, and it often suggests a different aspect of history from the one we were taught in school. In our history books we were told of the intrepid pioneer and his righteous cause in bringing civilization to the benighted Indians, yellow men, and blacks. The white man was the hero of the story—whether he was Vasco da Gama, Christopher Columbus, or Captain Cook—and his battle cry was *Dieu et mon droit.*

Here we have the colored man's reply; and it is, in the main, an extremely good-tempered reply.

The Sultan of Mysore may have reveled in his mechanical man-eating tiger (pages 20–21), but there is no attempt to caricature the unfortunate Englishman who is about to disappear into the animal's jaws. His eyes are wide and confiding, his hat is gallantly worn. The prosperous nabob in the Bengal painting (page 18) may be a trifle smug but he is not debauched, and the simpler African carvings generally represent the white man as a benign figure, almost a father-image.

Even more important than this is the quality of the work, not so much in the Japanese, Chinese, and Indian drawings —since there we would expect an accomplished technique —but in the African carvings. One has only to glance at the wooden figure (page 23) of the white nun in French Equatorial Africa to recognize a sculptural talent of great strength and feeling. The rapt and devoted woman is beautifully observed. It is very far indeed from the primitive mask which is usually associated with the tribes of central Africa. Even more remarkable are the famous Benin bronzes from West Africa. The sixteenth-century Portuguese musketeer on page 22 represents a degree of artistic skill which the invading Europeans certainly did not possess. The elaborate pattern on the helmet and the coat of mail is traced with a Renaissance freedom and exactitude; the stance is precisely that of a man about to lift a gun to his shoulder, and the hands are beautifully molded.

As they grew to know the white man better, the native artists appear to have followed a definite and logical progression in their work. The ship was the first evidence of the white man's arrival, and consequently it is the ship that recurs again and again in the early drawings of the coastal tribes around the world. We can even trace the development of Western navigation through native art: at first the sailing ship is depicted, then, in the nineteenth century, the paddle steamer with its auxiliary sails, and finally the modern oil-burning vessel driven by a screw. If today an expedition arrived at some still unexplored Shangri-La in New Guinea or on the upper Amazon, it would probably be the airplane which the native artist would fix on as the symbol of the white man. Ethiopia abounds with drawings showing the arrival of Italian bombers during Mussolini's invasion of 1935.

Next it was the men who landed from the ships who were noticed, and the emphasis was placed upon those things about them which seemed to the native to be distinctly peculiar: the high and broad-brimmed hats, the strange trousers and jackets, the boots, and the smoking pipes that protruded from the strangers' mouths. Since the Japanese and Chinese were small men, they tended to represent Europeans as very tall, massive, and hairy. Red hair amazed them to such an extent that they began to conceive that all Europeans were red-haired, or at any rate red-hair prone. Thus the Chinese term for white foreigners: "red devils."

In the early days there appears to have been very little attempt at direct portraiture. No doubt at first the native had difficulty in distinguishing one white man from another, and so he tended to represent them identically, like soldiers in uniform. (Might not our own artists do the same thing if the hordes from Mars ever did arrive?) Yet even in the most primitive work, it is not difficult to recognize the nationality of the Europeans who are depicted; the Frenchman's kepi is very clearly shown and so is the long face of the blond Englishman. In this respect, the native artists were hardly inferior to their European contemporaries. The engravings published in most of the explorers' books in nineteenth-century Europe make all blacks look pretty much the same, and there is a general tendency to exaggerate their wildness and fierceness. "Blackamoors" was a generic term, and a round woolly head with two round white-rimmed eyes was taken as a fair likeness of Africans and of South Sea Islanders as well.

The gun, of course—whether the antique musket or the newer rifle—is a major theme in native illustration of the whites. The gun set the white man apart; it was his special and terrible magic, the source of his devastating power. Its details are drawn with the greatest attention: hammer, lock, barrel, and butt. Possibly there may have been an ulterior motive here: it is one of the most widespread beliefs of primitive peoples—and not such a farfetched one at that—that by drawing an object or making a model of it you can to some extent possess it and exorcise its magic.

After the gun, other details come in, and we enter the stage where the native artist becomes familiar with white men—familiar enough to give separate individuals the sort of half-mocking and gleeful nicknames that school children attach to their teachers and to observe their foibles and their habits. In Africa the settler is increasingly shown with bottle and glass in hand; considerable attention is given to the details of his clothing—his buttons and buttonholes, for instance—to the cut of his beard, and to the umbrella he carries to protect himself from the tropical sun and rain.

This is the period when definite portraits of individuals appear. The west African figure of the nineteenth-century sailor (page 23) is undoubtedly a portrait, and so is the hookah-smoking Bengal colonist of somewhat earlier date. The more advanced Indian and Far Eastern artists were naturally much quicker to recognize the Europeans' failings than their simple African contemporaries were, but it is still not an unfriendly picture.

Portraiture of white women seems to have posed for the early African artists a problem they never quite overcame. It was seldom that a white woman accompanied the explorers and the military expeditions, and consequently she was a rarity. But even when she did arrive with the missionaries and the first settlers, the white woman was not easy to portray. Her voluminous clothes made it difficult for the artist to know the physical details of her body, and no doubt he was prepared to expect anything from the denizens of the outer world. Then, too, one must remember that a woman occupied a decidedly inferior position in tribal life; whether white or black, she was hardly a worthy subject for the artist. It was the man who had the power. Thus in many of the early native drawings and carvings she makes her rare appearances swathed in skirts that reach to the ground, almost bustless and hipless, and her face very often might be the face of a man.

There are exceptions of course. Nothing could be more delightful than the mischievous wood carving (page 23) of a teacher in French West Africa. Here is the schoolmistress we all know, spinsterish, strait-laced, disapproving—and yet we have a great affection for her. The large ears are certainly unkind, and perhaps the nose and the mouth are exaggerated, but all the rest we recognize instantly from the fashions of *la belle époque:* the straw hat, the high collar, the ruffles on the blouse, the muttonchop sleeves, the wasp waist, and the narrow skirt. She comes, of course, from Paris and the Seine, but alas, one feels she never attended any of those rip-roaring Maupassant summer-evening parties on the river; she was right here in the Tropics trying to teach these woolly-headed little brats (whom she loved) the Code Napoléon.

In the Far East, as well, we notice a certain division between the artist's treatment of his own and white women. His own, whether she be Japanese geisha or Moslem houri, is all grace, airiness, and delicate sensuousness. One is never left in an instant's doubt that her role in life is to please men. The white woman seen through Far Eastern eyes is a more formidable figure. It is true that in the picture of the American couple looking at the monkey (page 29), the lady has been given a pert and lively face and a cluster of roguish curls that peep out of her bonnet, but she grasps her walking stick in a way no geisha could ever do, and her crinoline is the height of fashionable decorum.

In the main, we have been dealing here with the first or, at any rate, the early contacts between whites and colored men. It was the period of innocence, of unself-consciousness, of experiment, and of intense curiosity. The native artist was still true to his own environment; he observed directly and without fear, and because he had no knowledge of other skills and cultures that were more sophisticated than his own, he did not imitate.

This was just a brief interlude in the world, and it could not possibly last. The colored artist, once he made contact with the whites, soon saw that he must put his innocence and his tribal life behind him and accept in exchange what Professor Lips called the "doubt and calculation" implicit in the feverish life of the white world.

The colored races no doubt have a good deal to reproach us with in our dominion over them through the seventeenth, eighteenth, and nineteenth centuries; and the loss of so much of their native art has certainly been one of the serious casualties, even though they have willingly connived at it themselves—at least to the extent of debasing their art by trying to please the European patrons and, more latterly, the hordes of tourists. The tide, however, has now turned. As the Red Indian GI is supposed to have exclaimed as he landed on the Normandy beaches on D-day, "Columbus, here I come!" In the past decade, India, Burma, and vast areas of Africa have won their independence, and the white man has been obliged to retreat from China and much of southeast Asia. Perhaps we are soon to see a new sort of pictorial art: the impression of the white artist recording the colored invasion—a peaceful invasion we hope—of the West.

Meanwhile it is pleasant to glance at these souvenirs of the first contact between the two groups of races and to know that the colored man so often looked upon the whites not too unkindly, not as a threatening monster but as an enlightened and benevolent extension of himself.

Alan Moorehead is an Australian author and journalist now living in Italy, whose experiences as a war correspondent have taken him into far corners of the world. Author of many books, including Gallipoli *and* The Russian Revolution, *his latest,* No Room in the Ark, *tells of wild game in Africa.*

The Image of the White Man in the Art of Other Races

A PORTFOLIO
ASSEMBLED AND DESCRIBED BY

JOHN MAASS
Visual Presentation Director of the City of Philadelphia and author of *The Gingerbread Age*

The Portuguese traders arriving in Japan after 1542 were greeted with great enthusiasm by the curious populace. In this detail from a seventeenth-century screen, a Portuguese sailor, painted with slightly Oriental features, is playing Go *with his Japanese guests on the sterncastle of his ship.*

In Seventeenth-Century Japan

An air of excitement hovered over Japanese ports when the black Portuguese carrack arrived on its yearly voyage from Macao. This scene shows Portuguese sailors resting after the journey while Indian deck hands furl the sails. On shore, the Portuguese captain, shaded by a parasol like any Eastern potentate, supervises the unloading of Chinese silks, gold, and trinkets onto a small skiff. A tall Negro in the foreground carries ivory tusks, a precious part of the cargo. Other traders pass a neat row of Japanese textile and porcelain shops,

BOSTON MUSEUM OF FINE ARTS

whose proprietresses peer eagerly at the new wares.

This "Southern Barbarian" screen of the Kano school was painted in the early seventeenth century, when the Portuguese enjoyed a profitable Japanese trade which was soon to end. The screens were so called because the foreigners who first sailed to Japan from the south struck the courteous Japanese as having little refinement. The features of the Portuguese which most impressed the artist were their billowing pantaloons and capes and their fierce black mustaches. Scenes like this were popular with the Japanese merchants who grew rich from their contacts with the Western traders.

The Portuguese were finally expelled from Japan in 1638 because of the overzealous missionary work of the Jesuits who accompanied them and the resistance of their Christian converts to the power of the shogun. Except for a handful of Dutch traders, the country was tightly closed off from the outside world for more than two hundred years—when Admiral Perry forced the reopening of Japan to the West.

In British India

The first settlers to arrive with the East India Company were quick to adopt the customs and delights of the land. The Bengal miniature at left, painted about 1760 by Dip Chand, shows a rather pompous settler smoking a hookah and attended by his servants in the manner of an Indian maharajah. He is thought to be Dr. William Fullarton, a Scot from Ayrshire. Fullarton was second surgeon at Fort William and the bane of company officials, who condemned him for mixing too freely with the Indians.

By 1858, the British had established complete rule in India and a court system with judges appointed by the Crown. In the new Kalighat style of painting, an actual Calcutta murder trial is portrayed (right). A Hindu priest had seduced a pretty Indian girl. Her jealous husband decapitated her and was promptly tried for murder. The detached trunk and head of the girl, still wearing arm jewelry and earrings, lie as evidence before the baby-faced English judge wearing the top hat which the bazaar artists associated with the British. The husband (left foreground), wearing a white dhoti, is held by a local policeman, while the bearded priest tells his story in the witness box. The fate of the unfortunate husband rests on the outcome of the contest being waged between the defense and the prosecuting attorneys behind him.

PRIVATE COLLECTION OF DR. O. W. SAMSON, LONDON

Tipu's Tiger

This Indian tiger gnawing at the neck of a helpless British colonel was the six-foot "toy" of Tipu Sahib, sultan of Mysore. It was captured at Seringapatam in 1799 and dispatched as a trophy of battle to the Court of Directors of the East India Company with the following memorandum: "This piece of Mechanism represents a Royal Tyger in the act of devouring a prostrate European. There are some barrels in imitation of an Organ, within the body of the Tyger, and a row of Keys of natural Notes. The sounds produced by the Organ are intended to ressemble the Cries of a person in distress intermixed with the roar of a Tyger. The machinery is so contrived that while the Organ is playing, the hand of the European is often lifted up, to express his helpless and deplorable condition."

The owner of this ingenious automaton was the son of Haidar Ali, who made Mysore the strongest state in India and the chief obstacle to the expansion of British rule. The father named his son "Tipu," which means "tiger" in Canarese, and he grew up to sit on a tiger throne and dress his army in striped tiger jackets. "Better to live two weeks as a tiger," Tipu was fond of saying, "than a lifetime as a lamb."

The automaton was built at the time of the Mysore wars,

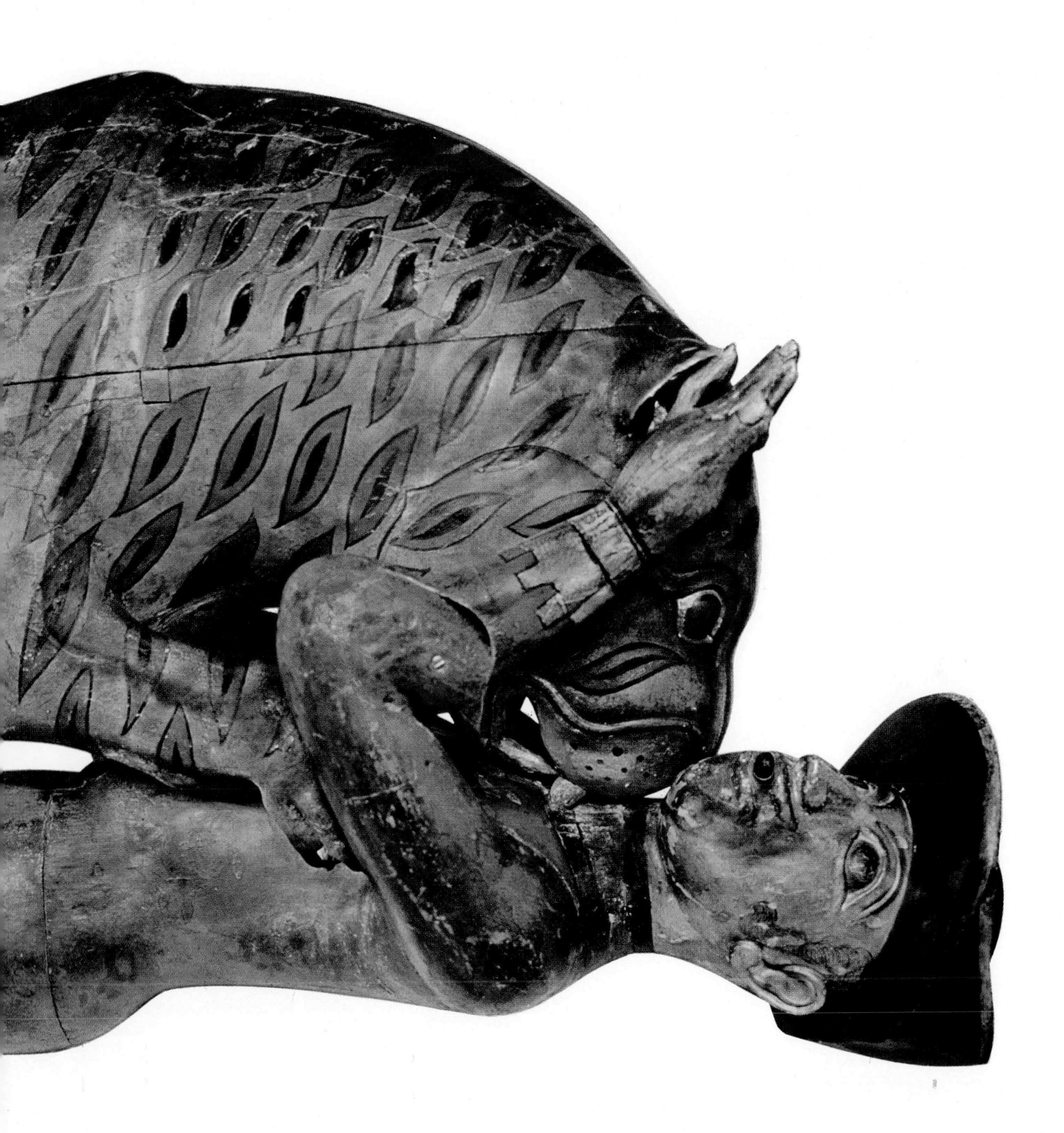

in which the British seized over half of Tipu's realm and held two of his sons as hostages. The interior mechanism, with its semi-mechanical pipe organ, was very likely manufactured by French craftsmen, for the French were Tipu's allies against the British, and automatons were at that time the rage in France. In any case, the musical tiger became the symbol of Tipu's consuming hatred of the British and of his desire for revenge. It is easy to imagine him sitting in the music room of the palace while a servant turned the crank on the tiger's left side, listening with delight to the growls of his favorite animal and the screams of his favorite victim.

Tipu died as he had lived. When a British army under General Sir David Baird stormed his fortress at Seringapatam, he was shot down, sword in hand, at the palace gate. The musical tiger was the chief prize in a shipload of trophies sent back to England. It ended up in the Victoria & Albert Museum where it has delighted generations of visitors, including John Keats. In his satiric poem The Cap and the Bells, *Keats describes a visitor to "mid-most Ind" who*

". . . feared less
A dose of senna-tea or nightmare Gorgon
Than the Emperor when he play'd on his Man-Tiger-Organ."

BY COURTESY OF THE TRUSTEES OF THE BRITISH MUSEUM

On the Coast of Africa

To the African, the gun was the power of the white man. The bronze statue of a sixteenth-century musketeer (left) was cast in Benin on the Slave Coast, after the Portuguese had arrived a century earlier. But the natives were also aware of their weaknesses, and on an ivory box cover (below, left), two sailors are engaging in a personal fight. As the riches of Africa attracted other European nations, the human qualities of the white man were portrayed further. The wood panel below, carved in Nigeria about 1900, shows a British district commissioner making his rounds. As he jounces along in a basketlike chaise held aloft by bearers, he wears the queasy expression of a man who wishes the ride were over.

UNIVERSITY OF PENNSYLVANIA MUSEUM

BY COURTESY OF THE TRUSTEES OF THE BRITISH MUSEUM

The wooden figures of a schoolmistress from Dahomey on the Guinea coast and a nun from Brazzaville in French Equatorial Africa (below) record the determined faces of these women who came with the French settlers to educate and proselytize at the end of the nineteenth century. Sturdy women were not unfamiliar in Dahomey, for this was a land of Amazons, where battalions of women held the field. Farther down the west coast, a Loango carver shaped this drum supported by the figure of a sailor clutching his bottle and glass (right). Loango was a source of slaves for the New World, and any seaman waiting for his ship to be loaded with its human cargo of "black ivory" could have served as the carver's model.

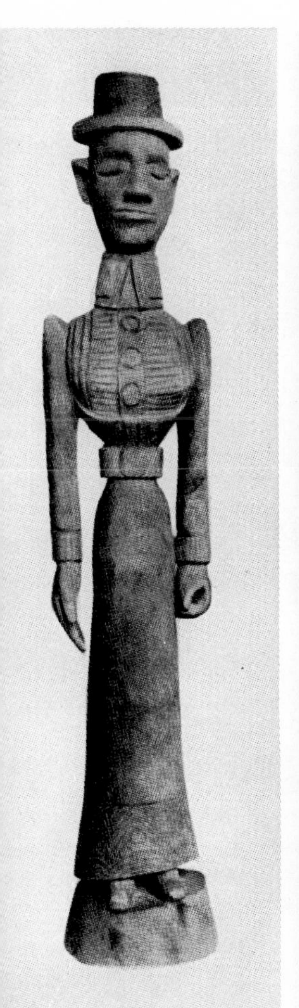

UTENSTRAUCH-JOEST MUSEUM, COLOGNE

UNIVERSITY OF PENNSYLVANIA MUSEUM

PEABODY MUSEUM, SALEM, MASS.

In Montezuma's Mexico

When the Spanish arrived in the Aztec kingdom in 1519, Montezuma sent artists to record the appearance of the mysterious strangers. The original parchments have since disappeared, but copies of these pictorial histories were made by Spanish priests. The entrance of Cortes is preserved in Codex Vaticanus Latinus 3738 (left) in which he appears as a bearded warrior, carrying the banner of the Holy Spirit in one hand and a long sword in the other. The Indians had never seen a horse, and the strange animal resembles a tall, panting dog with ears of a deer. From his capital of Tenochtitlan, Montezuma's envoy, represented by the feathered headdress glyph of the Aztec chief, brought gifts to bribe Cortes to turn back. When the Spanish refused, Montezuma had no recourse but to welcome them as his guests. A foreigner is already seen within the temple of Tenochtitlan, which is identified by the cactus glyph beneath that of Montezuma. The artist never doubted the intentions of the Spaniards, for below the rear leg of the horse, the shield and arrow glyph of war is clearly drawn.

An episode in the final conquest of the city two years later is told in Codex Azcatitlan (above), which reflects the European influence on the native Aztec style. The Spaniard Pedro de Alvarado fights off an Aztec while the wounded Cortes, who had fallen into one of the canals with other Spaniards, receives aid from a native ally.

In the Americas

The painted wooden medicine doll of a dour white man (far left) was carved by the Cuna Indians of San Blas, on the old Pirate Coast of Panama, to ward off illness. After the curing ceremony, these uchus *were thrown away.*

The artistic confusion of an angel with a gun (left) was also made by a San Blas carver, who gave it the wings of a Christian heavenly being along with the familiar weapon carried by the ubiquitous white tax collector.

The wishful dream of a North American Indian was drawn in his notebook with crayon colors (below). It shows the Cheyenne brave spearing a United States Cavalry officer. It was later found on his dead body after a fatal skirmish; a bullet had crumpled the right side.

The bearded effigy at right is the low man on a totem pole erected for the Haida Chief Skowl at Kasaan in the North Pacific in the 1880's. It is thought to be a likeness of the Austrian-born, Vincent Baronovich, who on a voyage north married the Chief's daughter.

MUSEUM OF THE AMERICAN INDIAN, NEW YORK CITY

BY COURTESY OF THE TRUSTEES OF THE BRITISH MUSEUM

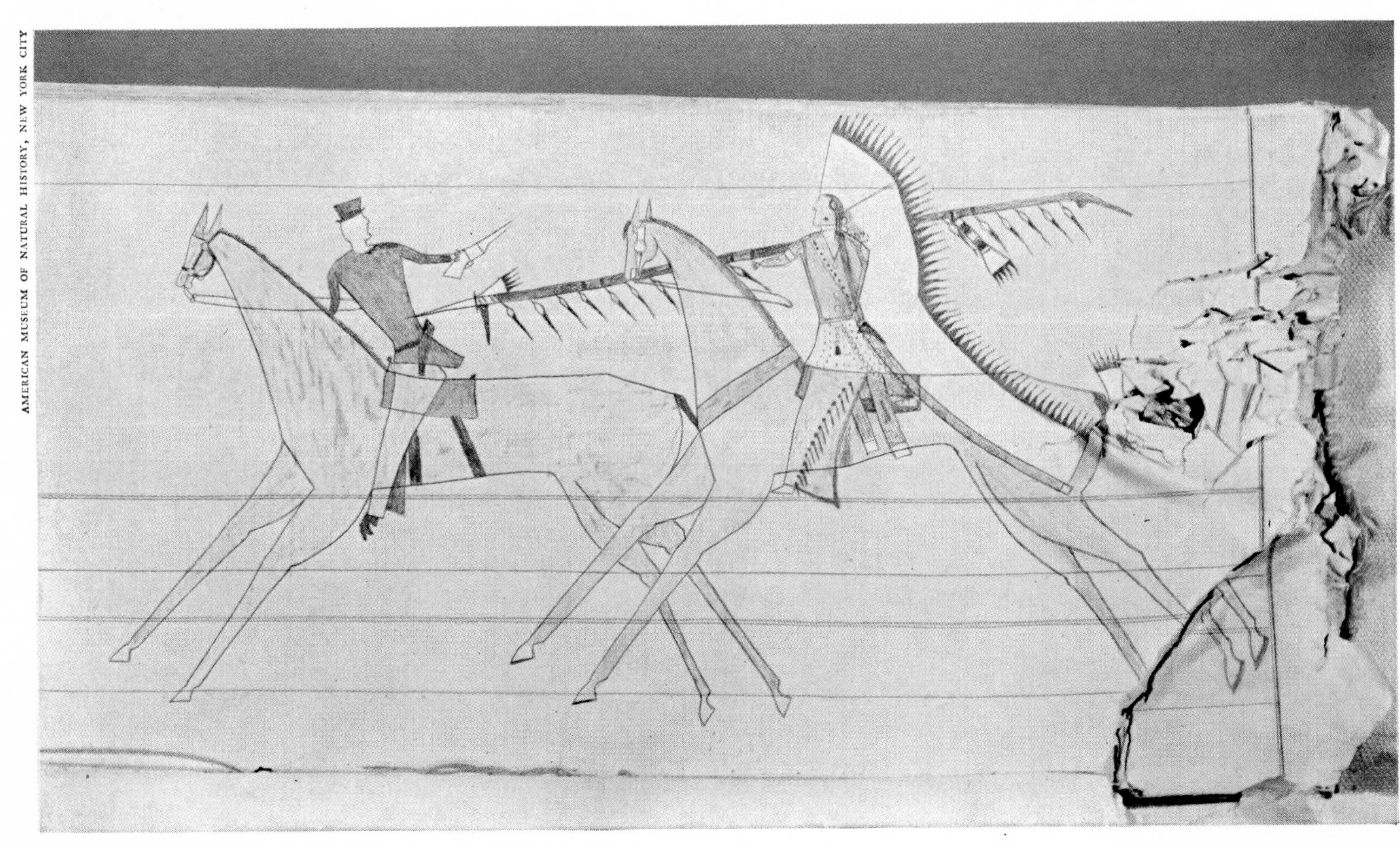

AMERICAN MUSEUM OF NATURAL HISTORY, NEW YORK CITY

OTTO SCHALLERER, KETCHIKAN, ALASKA

In China and Japan

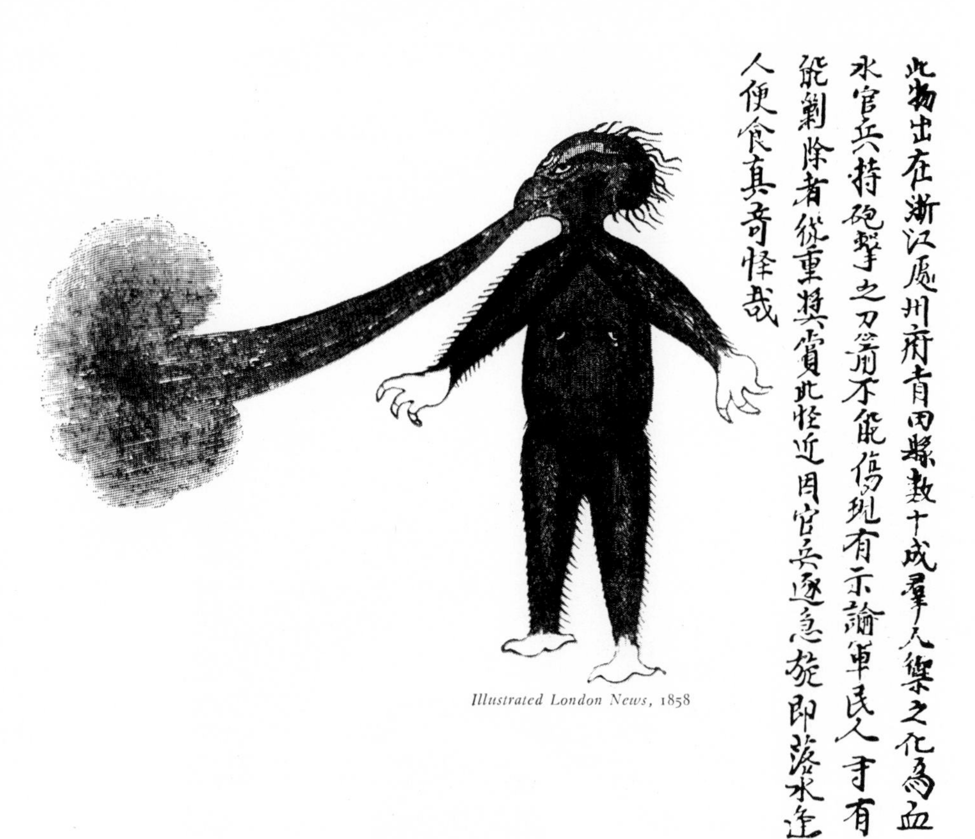

Illustrated London News, 1858

The hairy monster puffing smoke (left) was a mid-nineteenth-century caricature of a British sailor, meant as a deliberate insult to the Western intruders on Chinese civilization. The billowing cloud might represent the tobacco smoked by the sailors or the opium which was brought on the ships of the East India Company.

In calmer days a century earlier, a Chinese court artist painted on silk a band of musicians accompanying two Western dignitaries (below). Their features and tapering fingernails are Oriental, though their dress is Western. The scene was probably Canton, the only port open to foreign traders, where Chinese hong, or guild merchants, were appointed "For the continual instruction and guidance of the barbarians, and to repress their pride and profligacy."

After Japan was officially opened in 1854, Yokohama artists recorded the activities and types of foreign sightseers like the American couple on the opposite page viewing a monkey.

PRIVATE COLLECTION MR. & MRS. REGINALD PALMER, HURST, ENGLAND

天竺産尾長猿
一名ヲラウタン
アメリカ人
アメリカ女
横濱商家異人之圖
五雲亭貞秀画

Art by Accident

By LEONARD B. MEYER

Never before have artists let sheer happenstance paint their pictures or a throw of the dice shape their music—but then, never before have men tried so hard to avoid making decisions as they do now

ROBERT DESCHARNES; COURTESY *Art News*

Artistic creation has probably always involved accident. A melodic fragment hit upon by chance during improvisation or a street song overheard during an evening stroll has often been turned to good purpose by composers, both past and present. The accidental mixing of colors on a palette, the unforeseen flaw in a marble block have not infrequently influenced the final form of a painter's or a sculptor's work. Chance has always been with the creator as a condition of his occupation; it has been a fact of life to be accepted and turned to the artist's firm purpose. But chance has not until recently been elevated into a *principle* of creation.

Today a small but influential group of artists and musicians are intentionally using accident as a way of creating works of art. Jackson Pollock allowed chance to play an important role in his technique of painting. Placing his canvas on the floor, he trickled, poured, and dripped paint onto it from above in a series of freely improvised movements. The French painter Georges Mathieu attacks his canvas with frenzied gestures. Paint is squirted on the canvas from the tube, thrown at it, sloshed on it. As described by one art critic, Mathieu is "a true pentathlon artist [who] knows the full expressionist gamut: the spatter, the drip, the scumble, the drag, the pitch, and in some pictures he uses these all together in a free-for-all scrimmage." The end product of this violent assault is, to a considerable extent, the result of capricious chance.

It has been suggested by apologists for the accidental in art that this seemingly spontaneous, unreflective process of creation is not really accidental at all. Rather, it involves the use of the unconscious. Such aesthetic improvisations, they assert, allow the artist to express his innermost being—his unconscious image processes—free from the controlling restrictions of the ego or the superego.

The difficulty with this pseudo-Freudian account is that musicians, too, have of late elevated chance into a principle of creation. But since it is difficult to trace tonal patterns to unconscious image processes or repressed fantasies, this does not seem a plausible explanation for the composers' use of chance. Indeed, their dependence on accident has been so studied and blatant as to leave no doubt about their intentions in the matter.

John Cage, for instance, after assigning numbers to the tones of the scale, used the throws in a Chinese dice game (and, as will become apparent, it is significant that the game was Oriental) to determine the succession of pitches in one of his compositions. It is hard to see how the resulting music could in any way express Mr. Cage's unconscious. The German composer Karlheinz Stockhausen has allowed chance, usually in the form of the whim of the performer, to determine the order in which the parts of his compositions are to be played. For instance, his composition *Nr. 7 Klavierstück XI* (a portion of which appears on page 123) consists of nineteen musical fragments which are to be played in a more or less random order, according to the choice of the performer.

Here are some of Stockhausen's instructions to the pianist:

The performer looks at random at the sheet of music and begins with any group, the first that catches his eye; this he plays, choosing for himself tempo (small notes [which are to be played as fast as possible] always excepted), dynamic level, and type of attack. At the end of the first group, he reads the tempo, dynamic, and attack indications that follow, and looks at random to any other group, which he then plays in accordance with the latter indications.

"Looking at random to any other group" implies that the performer will never link up expressly-chosen groups or intentionally leave out others.

Each group can be joined to any of the other 18: each can thus be played at any of the six tempi and dynamic levels and with any of the six types of attack. . . .

When a group is arrived at for the third time, one possible realization of the piece is completed. This being so, it may come about that certain groups are played once only or not at all.

While one might conceivably argue that the *performer's* unconscious made him play one fragment rather than another, it is difficult to believe that Stockhausen's repressed image processes are themselves involved. Other composers have used tables of random numbers or the flip of a coin to choose their tonal, rhythmic, and thematic materials. Here chance rules directly and absolutely—the id, the ego, and the superego are in no way involved.

Until now the technique of creation by chance has, to the best of my knowledge, been confined to music and the plastic arts. Why not literature? Because literature employs an artificial system of signs, whose vocabulary, grammar, and syntax are almost entirely conventional. Consequently, the use of accident—for instance, rolling dice to choose letters or words—would give rise to obviously meaningless combinations. A semblance of spelling, vocabulary, and grammar (as in Lewis Carroll's "Jabberwocky") must be maintained if there is to be any communication at all. If chance enters, it can do so only on higher structural levels, such as those involving sequences of thoughts or events.

Visual and aural experience, on the other hand, can be unorganized and random and not *seem* totally meaningless. For one thing, the need of the human mind for order is so great that it will organize even random stimuli into some sort of pattern, if it possibly can. And in music and art, where the system of signs is less rigidly specified than in language, apparent pattern may arise out of accidental relationships. Moreover, though not strictly speaking intelligible, random music and art may be *suggestive*—in much the same way that Chinese poetry may seem suggestive (but not intelligible) when heard by someone who does not understand the language.

What are the reasons for the development of a technique based almost wholly on accident? Why should it attract

'n helmet and cross-leggings, Georges Mathieu refights—and paints—the Battle of Bouvines

artists and composers? Is it an isolated phenomenon, or is it related to other aspects of contemporary culture?

In a provocative article in *The Reporter* (March 6, 1958), Roger Maren argued that the use of accident as a principle of composition is essentially a reflection of the composer's unwillingness to make decisions—to make personal moral commitments. If the tones and rhythms of a piece of music are selected by flipping a coin, or the shapes of a painting are produced by hurling paint at a canvas from a distance, then the work of art is, in a sense, only *partly* the artist's responsibility. At least some part of the result can be attributed to chance. Or if the artist wishes to rationalize by asserting that he was guided by unconscious fantasies, then the psychoanalysts will assure him that he cannot be held responsible for those either. He does not have to account to the real arbiter, himself, for this particular note or that particular pattern. They just happened.

Maren observed that the use of accident is not the only way of avoiding decisions. Paradoxically, the exact opposite of using chance—adherence to an absolutely rigid set of rules—also tends to minimize the necessity for making decisions. The composer who bases every tone or progression—his whole composition, in fact—upon a single mathematical ratio, no less than the artist who employs a single geometric relationship for his painting, has imposed limits upon the kinds and numbers of decisions he must make. Thus it is not surprising to learn that the same composers who have made use of accident in their compositions—for instance, Stockhausen—have also written totally ordered music using a formula ("serial technique") which predetermines every single detail of the composition: pitches, rhythms, loudness, timbre, and so on.

This fear of decision-making—of individual responsibility—is not confined to the arts. It can be found in many areas of our cultural life. For instance, the tendency to have decisions made by groups—whether they be called "teams," as in Washington or at General Motors, or "committees," as they are in academic circles—is evidence of this trend. Of course, people have always worked together in reaching decisions. But until recently they have done so not for the purpose of making the decision itself but only in order to gather information upon which a single individual might base a reasonable decision. And it is perhaps no accident that for the first time, at least to my knowledge, music has been created by "co-operating" composers (Otto Luening and Vladimir Ussachevsky).

Or, to take another instance, David Riesman's "other-directed" man is, in a sense, one who also yields his prerogative (one might contend, his *obligation*) to make decisions. He allows the opinions of others to dictate his behavior, direct his decisions, and determine his preferences. Here again, it is not so much the phenomenon which is new—man has probably always been concerned with the opinions of others (see Polonius's instructions to Laertes)—what is different is the degree to which choices are now based upon the desire to conform.

The reliance on mathematical theories of games and strategy, which makes it possible to calculate the results of alternative courses of action and to choose among them, is further evidence of the uncertainty we feel in the face of difficult decisions. We are on the threshold, if indeed we have not crossed it, of the day when we shall be able to feed facts and figures—the pros and cons of a military situation, for instance—into a computer and have it decide what should be done: whether to advance or retreat, fight or surrender.

The interest of these artists and composers in Zen Buddhism is another indication of the appeal of the decisionless world. For Zen Buddhism is a religious philosophy that avoids decision-making. Alan Watts, one of Zen's most articulate spokesmen in this country, has observed that Zen requires *mushin*, a kind of inspired spontaneity. "It is," he wrote, "the art of making the appropriate responses to life without the interruption of that wobbling and indecisive state we call 'choosing.' "

Why has decision-making become such a formidable, traumatic business? The answer lies, at least in part, in the rapid, dramatic breakdown of the social, ethical, and aesthetic norms upon which behavior and choice have depended since the end of the Renaissance. This breakdown of tradition has enormously increased the number of decisions which must be consciously made. Tradition no longer limits our choices as it once did. To take an example from music: suppose that Bach wanted to harmonize the tone C in a piece in that key. Having once chosen the mode—major or minor—in which he would write, Bach had only four or five possible ways of harmonizing the tone, and the implications of each for subsequent musical development were quite clearly established by the norms of the style. Today, however, the same tone may be harmonized in dozens of different ways, and the implications of any particular harmonization are almost countless. Though some contemporary composers have found it possible to modify the rules of traditional practice, adapting them to present needs, others have been unable or unwilling to rely on modifications of traditional stylistic practice. The members of this latter group have tended to hedge their decisions with such an array of self-imposed rules that choosing is unnecessary. Or they leave it all to chance and flip a coin. They decide not to decide.

Even major changes in a value system, however, do not necessarily create a moral void. Values may seem confused for a time; new ones will conflict with the old and, if judged by past standards, may often appear false. But it is the task of educated men and women to try to understand the new as well as the old, to put changes in their proper perspective, and then to judge them dispassionately.

Let us therefore put aside, at least for the moment, our distaste for the notion of an art created by chance and try

CONTINUED ON PAGE 121

By JOHN KENNETH GALBRAITH

THE MUSE AND THE ECONOMY

When men are fighting tooth and nail for a living, they look on the arts as a thing apart. Has our affluent society today carried over some of this disdain into a time in which it really needs the artist and can gain from him as from the scientist?

Several years ago at a leading eastern university, the case arose of a young assistant professor of economics. He was an able and even brilliant teacher. He had written a number of good papers. One or two in particular showed originality, technical virtuosity, and incomprehensibility, a combination which is held in the highest professional regard. But he had grave drawbacks. These included a passion for music and painting and a morbid disinterest in the ordinary manifestations of material well-being. He lived in evident contentment in a small house heated by a coal stove. It was sensibly decided—though, it must be said, not without discussion—that he had no future as an economist. He was not promoted.

The incident illustrates the traditional relationship between art and economics.

There is none. Art has nothing to do with the sterner preoccupations of the economist. The artist's values—his splendid and often splenetic insistence on the supremacy of aesthetic goals—are subversive of the straightforward materialist concerns of the economist. He makes the economist feel dull, routine, Philistine, and uncomfortable—and also sadly unappreciated for his earthy concern for bread and butter, including that which nourishes the artist. Not only do the two worlds not meet, but the regret in each is evidently negligible.

Increased means and increased leisure are the two civilizers of man.
Benjamin Disraeli

This alienation, though unregretted, is unfortunate. The economist can perhaps say something to the artist about his environment and what is agreeable to the artistic imagination. And the artist stands in far more important relation to economics—and indirectly to politics—than we have yet realized. I shall end this essay by arguing that one of the more important problems of our day—the weakening of the American balance of international payments and the complex of foreign and domestic issues which follow in its train—is partly the result of the alienation of the artist from our economic life. But first a word or two of explanation.

The amateur venturing into the world of art is soon made to feel the perils of his path. Art is both the creation of beauty and its language. But art and how to deal with Russia have this in common: that subjectivity is the parent of both certainty and emotion. One man's beauty, it is clear, is another man's missed opportunity; had the critics been present at the time, there would have been some highly deprecatory words about the Lord's creative instinct. I shall not venture to say what is beauty; and fortunately for the purposes of this essay, I need only to be allowed a certain band within which it will be agreed that it occurs. Whether a particular artist or work belongs within this band is not something I need decide.

I have need to refer not only to the artist but to those for whom his language has meaning. This is the community which shares the artist's imagination and responds to it. Its size and the depth and discernment of its response are matters of much importance. I shall refer to it simply as the aesthetic response.

The economic myth of the artist is that of a man devoid of material baggage and indifferent to pecuniary reward. It is not a myth that can be reconciled entirely with reality. In the Graeco-Roman epoch, the painter or sculptor soiled his hands at a wearisome and hence unbecoming toil. Accordingly, and unlike the poet, he was identified with the artisan and the slave, and his pay was that of a worker. This was only slightly less true of the early Renaissance artists: Arnold Hauser describes them in his *Social History of Art* as "economically on a footing with the petty bourgeois tradesman." However, by the latter part of the fifteenth century, the great painters had, financially speaking, come into their own. Raphael and Titian lived handsomely on ample incomes. Michelangelo was a wealthy man; it was because of his wealth that he was able to decline payment for the design of St. Peter's. Leonardo ultimately received a handsome salary.

The mother of the practical arts
is need;
that of the fine arts
is luxury.
Schopenhauer

In later times it is difficult to make a rule. The Dutch masters, as a consequence of heavy overproduction, had a hard time. Rembrandt, Hals, and Vermeer led a financially precarious existence. For what we would now call reasons of economic security, Van Goyen traded in tulips, Hobbema was a tax collector, and Jan Steen was an innkeeper. In modern times Van Gogh, Gauguin, and Toulouse-Lautrec were vagabonds because this was implicit in their alienation from bourgeois civilization. But interspersed through the history of Western painting from Rubens to Picasso have been others—including Americans—who have earned great fortunes. Copley was rich enough to speculate in real estate and owned much of Beacon Hill. Winslow Homer lived a very comfortable life. The most popular of the abstract expressionists are being handsomely rewarded by any standards. It is not clear that wealth has been or is an insuperable obstacle for the artist.

What is not in doubt is that the aesthetic response is nourished by secure well-being. From classical Athens through the princes, bankers, and popes of the Renaissance, the Dutch bourgeois of the seventeenth century, the courtly patrons of the seventeenth and eighteenth centuries to the collectors and connoisseurs of modern times, wealth has been the unmistakable companion of art. Perhaps it has not always brought a discerning interest. But if it has not been a sufficient influence, it certainly has been a facilitating one. The artist may transcend hunger and privation—conceivably his senses are honed by suffering. But not so his audience. It turns to art after it has had dinner. At first glance, such a Philistine assertion will surely seem suspect. But, subject always to individual exceptions, it will hardly be argued that the aesthetic response has been as strong from the poor and the insecure as from the rich and established. As Edward D. Stone has remarked, "Great periods in art have traditionally come with stability in government, with prosperity and leisure."

One can bring these matters within the scope of a simple hypothesis. It is that pecuniary motivation—roughly, the desire for money income—has a marked tendency to pre-empt the individual's emotions. Only as it releases its grip is there opportunity for artistic or, for that matter, any cultural or intellectual interest not immediately related to income. As Alfred Marshall observed in his *Principles of Economics,* "The business by which a person earns his livelihood generally fills his thoughts during by far the greater part of those hours in which his mind is at its best." If he and his family live under the threat of hunger, cold, or exposure, this preoccupation will be total. By the same token, to remove the threat of physical hardship will be, other things equal, to weaken the role of pecuniary motivation and allow other influences to enter the pattern of life.

The best and clearest thinking
of the world is done
and the finest art is produced,
not by men who are hungry,
ragged and harassed,
but by men who are well-fed,
warm, and easy in mind.
It is the artist's first duty
to his art to achieve
that tranquility for himself.
H. L. Mencken

The fear of hardship, we may assume, will play somewhat the same pre-emptive role as hardship itself. And fear is not confined to physical hardship. As most people are constituted, they will be perturbed by any serious threat to existing levels of well-being. They defend accustomed living standards with considerable tenacity. Accordingly, if people are so circumstanced that they live under the threat of a reduction in income—of being plunged into some dark and half-imagined abyss—pecuniary motivation will be strong. The gods are waiting to hurl the unwary to his doom; they can only be propitiated by unremitting vigilance. The secure man, in contrast, can turn his thoughts to other matters.

Until comparatively recent times, the preferred model of a nonsocialist society was one of marked uncertainty. Production was for a common market made by many sellers; in this market, prices moved freely in response to changes in consumer taste or need or changes in cost and output. Incomes, at least in the form of profits, salaries, or wages, were inherently insecure. Favorable profits, for example, would attract new participants. This was possible because entry into any business was assumed to be inexpensive and easy. The resulting increase in supply would lower prices and therewith profits, and, in practice, the unco-ordinated response of numerous new entrants could easily cause profits to disappear. Profits could also disappear as the result of unexpected or inexplicable shifts in consumer taste or changes in technology, which gave other producers a sudden and substantial advantage in cost. Wages and salaries shared the uncertainty of the income from which they came.

The uncertainty of this model, it should be noted, was not only intrinsic but a virtue. It was what punished sloth and kept producers on their toes. This is almost exactly to say that the system was designed to make pecuniary motivation as nearly pre-emptive as possible. It was meant to be artistically barren, for it rewarded a full-time concern with making money, and it drove its participants with the omnipresent possibility of failure.

The nearest approach to the competitive model in the American economy is agriculture. Here many comparatively small producers do supply a common market under conditions which, in the past at least, have been characterized by marked uncertainty. In this industry, earnings often have suddenly and disastrously disappeared for many participants. Without stopping to consider the reason, we expect the modern practicing farmer to be beyond the reach of the aesthetic response. That the successful lawyer should have a concern for painting does not surprise us. But not the successful cattleman. He is the man for whom the calendars and the *Saturday Evening Post* covers are drawn. As his income increases, he may develop an interest in a better automobile, possibly in an airplane, and certainly in an array of consumer goods. That he should develop a serious concern for painting or sculpture or even for domestic architecture is not expected. A farmer has too many other worries. He cannot be frivolous or eccentric. Unlike the more secure lawyer, it is taken for granted that his pecuniary concerns are pre-emptive.

As with the farmer, so generally with the small businessman—the dealer, salesman, contractor, and small merchant. His income may be handsome by any past standards. But he is a man who has to hustle. Accordingly, the arts are not for him. George Babbitt, who in secret moments hungered for something with slightly more magic, knew in the end that he had to keep his thoughts on the real-estate business. The competitive economy still imposes this requirement.

Were ours still an economy of insecure small producers, we would have therein a sufficient explanation for the alienation of art from economic life. The insecurity of such a society is pre-emptive; the aesthetic response will only be strong where it is somehow protected from the dominant economic motivation.

But, gentlemen, what would I want
with the original pictures
when the ones right here in these books
are so beautiful.
Henry Ford to Lord Duveen

But modern economic society does not conform to the competitive model. The centerpiece of the modern capitalist economy is the great corporation. It is an institution which is arranged to provide a rather large number of people with rather large and secure incomes. Through control of its prices and of its sources of supply, by diversification of its products, by research which ensures that technological innovation does not catch it unaware, and, in degree, by the management of consumer tastes, the modern corporation has either eliminated or much reduced the main sources of insecurity of the competitive firm. As a result, earnings are highly reliable: of the one hundred largest industrial firms in the United States, not one failed to earn a profit in 1957, and that was a year of mild recession.

Thus the modern corporate executive enjoys a security of income and tenure comparable with that of a college professor. In examining the protection which a vocation accords to the individual, one should examine the fate not of the successful but of the unsuccessful. The benign and protective character of government employment is indicated by the decorative sinecures into which the inadequate can be sidetracked with appropriate ceremony. Ambassadorships in untroubled countries, assistant secretaryships for public affairs, or membership on the Federal Communications Commission are all available. In colleges and universities, compassion is similarly manifested by establishing research projects to review progress in behavioral sciences or international relations, by appointing deans to handle relations with parents, wives, or the local churches, or by assigning committees to reconsider the curriculum. But the modern corporation is peculiarly rich in its arrangements for cushioning the fall of the man who stumbles in mid-career. Not only are a wide variety of posts—public relations, staff relations, community liaison, charitable contributions, supervision of office festivities—available with honorific titles but there is also in most firms an understanding, not present in the university, that all will deny fiercely that any featherbedding is involved.

Accordingly, the comparatively secure and remunerative life provided by the modern corporation should be hospitable to the arts. Eventually it will be; and for the good of the economy, it must so become. However, the myth of the insecure, tough, competitive enterprise has outlasted the reality. Business is still assumed to require a total concentration of energies; anything less is still deemed to be out of character. And men are still treated by their commitment, or by their simulation of a commitment, to what is held to be a demanding, no-nonsense, nose-to-the-grindstone, hard-driving existence. To suppose that the requirements of a business career are secondary, or supplementary, to artistic or cultural interests or to a means of supporting them is still the exception. There are distinguished exceptions, but they depart from the general rule. At the turn of the century, Charles Lang Freer made his business, as a builder of railroad cars, the servant of his interest in Whistler and Oriental art. His industrialist friends complained that he preferred talking about the tariff on paintings to discussing the price of steel. Such talk might still cause question about his effectiveness as a businessman.

Indeed, in all this one senses that there has even been a reversal of form. Two generations ago, with the highly interested assistance of Duveen, the great tycoons proved by their art collections that they were not mere moneygrubbers. A few million dollars invested in Botticelli, Fra Angelico, Rembrandt, or Vermeer showed, as nothing else, that the investor was identified with the secure and aristocratic leisured classes from the Renaissance on. Now the organization man may seek to prove the opposite. In his single-minded devotion to his enterprise, he shows that he is identified in spirit with the hard-bitten entrepreneurship but not with the other interests of Henry Clay Frick, Andrew Mellon, and J. Pierpont Morgan.

In the past, culture has been
paid for by the ruling classes;
they paid, but they paid,
much as they went to church;
it was the proper thing to do,
it was a form of social snobbery,
and so the artists sneaked a meal,
the author got a sinecure,
and the work of creation went on.

E. M. Forster

Modern Soviet painting—the socialist realism which depicts strong maidens looking to the sun over the high-yielding wheat—asserts that art is the handmaiden of economics. Its goal is to help organize the country for the maximum of aesthetically static output. Those who insist on the total primacy of economic motivation in our economic life come out curiously near the same point. They, too, are likely to insist on forthright realism and to defend it, not without indignation, as "what the people want." They may also, on occasion, be suspicious of what unduly taxes the imagination. The very painting which official Communist critics characterize as bourgeois degeneracy, the down-to-earth American conservatives condemn as Communist-inspired. Both, we may imagine, find it difficult to reconcile such art with pre-emptive pecuniary motivation. Although the need to defend it no longer exists, the habit persists.

To the extent that the business firm still insists on the primacy and inviolability of economic goals, it excludes and alienates the artist and narrows the aesthetic response normal to a society of secure well-being. There are three other ways in which the model of a competitive society, as it affects its corporate successor, is at odds with the artist. One of these, of particular importance to the architect, is its tendency to deny him control of the aesthetic environment. In the competitive model, the role of the state is slight. It is meant to be a self-regulating economic society in which the best government, in economic matters, governs the least. The modern corporate economy has found it convenient to assert the same rule wherever it is reasonably plausible, for it keeps public authority from intruding on the not unwelcome exercise of private authority. In the years following World War II, and partly no doubt in reaction to the wartime controls and the individuals who administered them, we had a strong resentment toward anything seeming to smack of centralized guidance of economic activity. "Planning" became an evil word. The uncontrolled development of economic activity was justified not only on grounds of efficiency. It became a moral good.

In Cambridge, Massachusetts, near the banks of the Charles, there are two buildings—an auditorium and a chapel—designed by Eero Saarinen. They are, one imagines, beautiful buildings, but no one can really know. For on one side is an early Norman-style apartment house and on the other a dingy four-story brick structure. In front is a parking lot filled with multicolored and often rather dirty cars; behind are a candy factory, a fireproof storage warehouse, and a large sign advertising the 57 Varieties. Down the road are purveyors of fried foods and gasoline. St. Mark's might well lose some of its charm were the Piazza San Marco surrounded by Gulf, Esso, and Jenney stations, and a Do-nut shop, with Howard Johnson's at the end. But such grotesque arrangements are strongly defended by the competitive ideology. They are the natural and valued consequence of competitive enterprise. The man who questions the outcome runs the risk of being called an impractical aesthete who has not properly grasped the principles which have made the system what it is today.

An object of art creates
a public capable of finding
pleasure in its beauty.
Production, therefore, not only
produces an object for the subject
but also a subject for the object.
Karl Marx

The second problem is advertising—not all of it but an important part. As people are less persuaded of their desires by physical need, someone is certain to seek to persuade them. The essence of this persuasion is to attract attention. This advertising does in one successful form by allowing beauty to attract our eyes or ears and then introducing a contrasting, which is to say, in practice, a jarring note. Thus advertising cannot seek harmony with its environment. The most beautiful billboards would be those that blended into the landscape—and were not seen. The most agreeable commercials would be those that did not interfere with the play or music—and were not heard. Such advertising, it will be contended, would be ineffective. But then it cannot be argued that the jarring alternatives are a contribution to beauty. In speaking of the pre-emptive tendencies of pecuniary motivation, I have been speaking of a force which alienates industry from the artist. Advertising—that which is juxtaposed to beauty—has the equal but opposite effect. It alienates the artist from industry. Possibly it is the most important influence determining the reaction of the artist to economic life.

Finally there is the conflict in which the modern industrial firm finds itself, under the best of circumstances, between the pursuit of sales and the pursuit of excellence. Few would wish to argue that the popular taste is the best taste—that it reflects the highest aesthetic response. And it is quite clear that the ordinary industrial firm must produce for the popular market. Thus there may be, by the artist's standards, a deliberate preference for commonplace or banal design. But the businessman, in the first instance at least, is hardly to be blamed. When the Court and a few cultivated Parisians provided the principal market for French craftsmen, the standard of artistic excellence could be high. The standard would certainly have fallen if France had suddenly become a prosperous, egalitarian democracy.

The business of America is business.
Calvin Coolidge

It seems probable, however, that modern industrial design has managed to get the worst of a bad bargain. Taste is not static. And change begins with those who are in communication with the artist, those who have a strong aesthetic response. Industry, alienated from the artist and with its eyes fixed, by way of the market researchers, on the popular taste, has regularly failed to perceive those advances in taste which were rendering its designs banal and otiose. Instead of being a little ahead, it has usually been a little behind.

Progress toward better design has also been handicapped by planned obsolescence. To offset excessive durability and the inhibiting effects of this on demand, many products must be constantly restyled. These constant changes cannot but have an exhausting effect on the artistic resources of the industry. In the past, good design lasted for a long time—and this, one imagines, was one reason it was good.

In a diverse society such as ours, economic institutions are not coterminous with life; there is much room for development in the interstices. Accordingly, the preemptive role of economic motivation and the associated problems of the competitive society are not fatally damaging to the artist or to the aesthetic response. Certainly they are far less damaging than in the Communist countries.

We have seen, moreover, that part of the hostility—the determined preoccupation with down-to-earth pecuniary concerns in the modern large corporation—is based not on necessity but on the perpetuation of a myth. The myth is not invulnerable. Without question, its hold is weakening. Of all artists, the architect is the most dependent on the aesthetic response. Its absence brings us an enormous amount of very bad building with which, no doubt, we will have to put up for a very long time. The glass beehives and shoddy metal boxes which disfigure Manhattan—long our proudest architectural exhibit—are perhaps the greatest tragedy. But even here there are brilliant exceptions, although—if there is need to prove a rule—they have been mostly cases where, fortuitously or otherwise, pecuniary motivation was not predominant. Rockefeller Center was built by an affluent family of marked aesthetic response and at least partly as a demonstration piece. In the United Nations group, commercial motivations were absent and the architects had an exceptionally free hand. The Lever Brothers Building was built by a company headed by an architect temporarily miscast as a businessman. The Seagram Building no doubt reflects the greater need of a distillery for ultimate distinction than for immediate gain, and also the sensitivity of an influential daughter to the work of Mies van der Rohe. And there are many instances—the General Motors Technical Center, Connecticut General's new buildings, and others—where corporations in the ordinary course of business have given rein to the artistic imagination.

The trouble, Mr. Goldwyn,
is that you are only interested in art
and I am only interested in money.
George Bernard Shaw

It is not the artist who has suffered from the alienation of art from economics but the reverse. For the economic system, the alienation is serious—more serious certainly than is imagined. In recent years there has been a sharp decline in the export of American goods. There has been an even more dramatic increase in the import of European-made products. As one result, the American balance of payments is weak—a brief episode in 1932–33 apart—for the first time in our modern history. In largest part, the problem is one of cost; for a considerable range of our goods, we have been pricing ourselves out of world markets, including our own. But in no small measure it is a matter of design: our goods have fallen below both European standards and our own tastes. It would seem that "the American people can afford everything but beauty." But, in fact, they have been searching for it with no small diligence, and they have been finding it in Italian, French, German, and Swedish products far more often than in our own. The automobile is the most important and also the most publicized example. But in a host of other products—furniture, glass, ceramics, leather, metalware—Americans have turned to foreign designs in the same way as foreigners have turned away from American products. As Edward D. Stone has pointed out, in their search for beauty our people have been turning away from the disorderly and billboard-studded American scene. This lies behind part of the annual tourist migration, which also has an effect on the balance of payments.

Our failure has not been general. There is much good American design. Industry in many fields has come into communication with the artist and has shown itself capable of a strong aesthetic response. But in an alarming number of instances, this clearly is not the case. In these industries it is supposed that industry is something apart from art or, at best, that the artistic imagination must be kept carefully subordinate to popular appeal. And here the customers have been responding to the closer identification of European industry with the artist, and vice versa, and to the superior product that results.

That design is one dimension of quality no one will question. But that it is a dimension of growing importance must still be stressed. A poor society may ask only that its products be well engineered; a richer one is certain to require that they have beauty as well. In the earlier stages of industrialization, the engineer is important. In the later stages he yields place to the artist. The practical man who holds that this is a lot of precious nonsense may, like the automobile makers, have to learn the truth the hard and expensive way.

Indeed one already senses that the learning is causing pain. One senses a kind of angry impatience over the rejection of various of our own products and the popularity of European replacements. This is something that is being put over by the highbrows and the cultural snobs. If the honest American had been left alone, he would have remained with his honest chrome. We are a brass-rail-and-cuspidor folk; we welcome a nice dashboard and a fancy decanter for our neutral grain spirits. The mark of an American is that he rises above any precious tendencies to look for beauty, especially in useful things. There is not much future in this kind of cultural protectionism. Self-criticism will probably stand us in better stead.

Art in the native American mind enjoys the dubious importance attached to the Devil in the medieval mind.
Alexander Harvey

To summarize, then: in a simple society, pecuniary motivation can be powerful and indeed transcendent. And perhaps it must be, for the earning of bread, where bread is scarce, has to be a preoccupying concern. But one of the happy consequences of security and reasonable well-being is that people have time and thought and emotion for other things. Economic institutions must, in turn, be responsive to this change. At least partly under the influence of the earlier myth, our institutions are less responsive than they should be. We are still reluctant, moreover, to accept the social and political arrangements, notably the planning, that would allow harmony between the artist and his environment. We are tolerant of the destruction of beauty if it sells the goods. Those who assail our senses or disfigure our landscape for commercial purposes can still presume to claim that they are serving the paramount goal of the society.

The artistic imagination enters only rather furtively into economic life. Artistic truth is still revealed not by the artist but by the market researcher. In a community of developing taste, he may be a guide only to the obsolescent.

The remedies are not simple. Pecuniary goals are unequivocal and direct. To avow and pursue them is an uncomplicated matter. To create beauty is anything but simple. The goals are highly equivocal—indeed it will regularly precipitate an awkward struggle over the nature of beauty. To recognize, as now we must, that society must assume responsibility for the protection of the aesthetic standards of the environment will bring bitter debate. So will the need to subordinate jarring salesmanship to aesthetic goals. And the American businessman, having accommodated himself to the scientist in the course of accommodating himself to the twentieth century, must now come to terms with the artist. Artistic perception is as necessary to the modern manufacturer of consumer goods as engineering skill. Indeed, now more so. How it is brought to bear is another—and long—story. But as a start, we can reject the myth that still holds that it has no place.

Economist, historian, former government official and Fortune *editor, John Kenneth Galbraith is the author of numerous books, including* The Affluent Society *and* The Liberal Hour, *to be published this fall—a collection in which this essay will appear.*

"The key to all is the SMILE"

OSBORN'S AMERICANS

Few are spared by this rough-riding satirist

Some years ago Robert Osborn illustrated a small book of mine. My secretary, fresh out of college, told me with evident pleasure that her contemporaries thought my text made an adequate accompaniment to Osborn's wonderful drawings. I wasn't exactly touched by this observation; it was my book, after all, not his. In recent years, however, there must have been a dozen authors who have had to admit to themselves, if they were honest, that Osborn had taken their raw material and crystallized it as they had been unable to do. I wonder how often in publishing houses some editor says to his colleagues, "What this book needs is Osborn."

But Osborn off on his own is better than Osborn pulling someone else's chestnuts out of the fire. The drawings (many already published, some not) that have been selected for this portfolio represent Osborn not just as an illuminator of other people's texts but mainly as a social critic on his own. They offer only one facet of Osborn, as anyone who has seen his work in magazines (and who hasn't?) knows, but it is the one that casts the most penetrating light and is most characteristic of him. It is not, however, the one that matters most to Osborn. Before he is a social critic, he is the engineer at the throttle of a pencil or a brush (to use his own kind of imagery), and his greatest pleasure is in driving the implement in his hand to do precisely what he wants it to do. Osborn is first an artist and second a satirist. If ever a society needed satirists who are also artists, ours does; and like every good satirist, Osborn bites the hand that needs him.

Happily for his friends, Osborn's public bite is a good deal worse than his private bark. He is a tall, generous man in his fifties, with graying brown hair; he laughs a good deal —a serious man with an unresting sense of the ridiculous. There is less contradiction than one might think in the fact that he is an uncommonly pleasant and enthusiastic man with a considerable talent for putting his pencil on the commonly unpleasant truths about our society. He is continually transmuting a general observation into a specific truth. He

By RUSSELL LYNES

"Middle-western businessman on the loose in New York City"

will interrupt a conversation with, "Say that again," and then, "Can't you just see it?" and he draws in the air with his hands, converting your statement into a visual image. And of course you do see it.

Osborn lives in a sort of bucolic idyll with his wife and two young sons on a hillside in the Berkshires near Salisbury, Connecticut, a slingshot from the Massachusetts line. But there is nothing nostalgic about the idyll. His house is modern, as much glass as white stucco; the pictures in it are by Klee and Miró and Shahn, and the sculpture is by Calder and Despiau and Lipchitz. His studio is a separate building, an elevated and balconied box fifty yards from the house. It looks down on his wife's garden, across a meadow and over the tops of evergreens to the hills. ("Dear God," he says, "did you ever see anything so beautiful as the way the light falls on that meadow?") When the wind is up in his fertile mind, he will sit all night in his studio and draw, strewing the floor with sketches as his hand becomes surer and the image grows simpler and sharper, funnier or more biting. "Look at this," he often says, holding a drawing. "Isn't that the damnedest thing? I don't know where it came from." He is constantly surprised at himself and frequently delighted.

It was the Navy that, in a sense, transmuted Osborn from the general to the specific. He was born in Oshkosh, Wisconsin, the son of a prosperous lumberman, and after he graduated from high school, he went briefly to the University of Wisconsin. As a juvenile his innards were delinquent (he knows more about ulcers than the businessmen he satirizes), and after a brief stay at Wisconsin, he spent six months in a Chicago hospital. Eager to see what he then considered the world, he persuaded his father to let him go east to Yale. From Yale, where he was art editor of the *Record*, he went to Rome to study painting. ("If you're going to be an artist," his father said to him, "learn to paint an apple so you want to bite it.") He then returned to teach at The Hotchkiss School (art, Greek philosophy, and football), an experience which hurried him back to Europe, this time to Paris to study with Despiau and Othon Friesz. As a painter of landscapes, nudes, and still lifes he did not, he felt, distinguish himself, but he did manage to get himself thrown into jail in Portugal for drawing cartoons on an official immigration

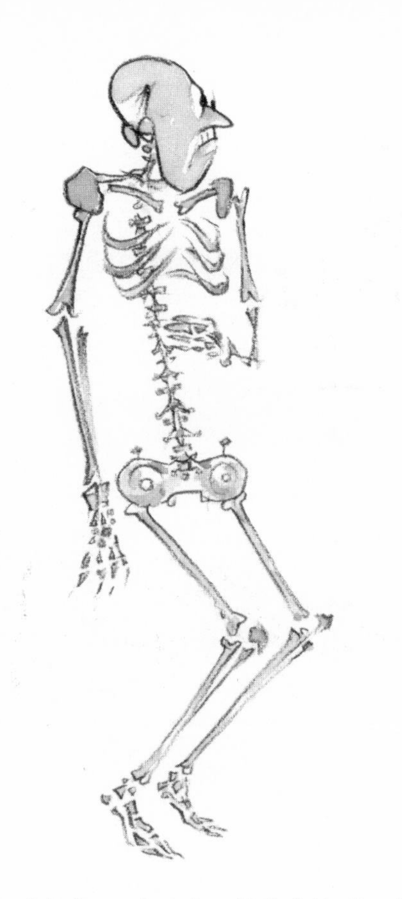

"At least there is a little left after Uncle Sam has taken his pound of flesh"

MACHINE AGE: *"The pressures build UP!"*

form. In 1939 he produced the first in a series of "caricature" books called *How to Shoot Ducks, How to Catch Trout,* etc., which sold surprisingly well. Then the war came and with it a commission in the Navy, for which he created a character named Dilbert, a pilot who made every mistake in the sky and who became as famous in naval air circles as Admiral Nimitz. Osborn had become a cartoonist.

But as demonstrated by his first book after his discharge, *War Is No Damn Good!* he had become something a good deal more deadly. He had become one of the most furious satirists of our time. In his hand a pencil had become a bull whip with which he struck out at pompousness and pretension, at human waste and indignity, at loss of individual identity, and at all kinds of simpering self-satisfaction. As the aim of his whip became more accurate, his visual images became more abstract and his sweeping line became surer and sharper and cut closer to the bone. Objects became men and beasts. The helmet became the soldier, the "S" in the dollar sign became a serpent, the T square became the architect. Since *War Is No Damn Good!* there have been two other books—*Low & Inside,* a civilian counterpart to the war book, and *Osborn on Leisure,* a homily on why-the-hell-are-we-beating-our-brains-out. There is about to be still another, *The Vulgarians,* aimed at our excesses and complacencies.

Subtlety is rarely a characteristic of Osborn's satire, although it is often a quality of his drawing. He is a master of overstatement. When he operates on the body politic, he exposes the heart and makes you see it bleed. Consequently the foibles of society are often exposed as deadly evils and its minor excesses as deadly sins. He frequently seems to strike with the same vehemence at the skin as at the core, and he sometimes hollers when a whisper would be more effective. But he is an artist who cares passionately about the private man—his dignity, his sense of adventure, his capacity for heroism and for fear. Osborn sees our society crushing, emasculating, and seducing this man with false blandishments of wealth and security, and he'll be damned if he'll whisper when he sees the express train of destruction roaring down the tracks of progress to crush his friends.

Russell Lynes, author of The Tastemakers, A Surfeit of Honey, *and other books, is, like Osborn, a searching social critic.*

MADISON AVENUE: *"The jab-sell"*

TELEVISION: *"Foaming nonsense"*

Osborn on popular institutions

In his newest book, *The Vulgarians* (from which the drawings opposite and below are taken, along with "SMILE," which opens this portfolio), the artist unlooses a barrage upon what he sees as the excesses of commercialism and the building of stock mass responses today. Yet, while a champion of individuality and the refuge of privacy, he also explores the intimacies of the home: witness the recent drawing at right.

MARRIAGE: *". . . till death do us part"*

ROADSIDE: *"The once endless beauty of our land . . ."*

Osborn on war and bureaucracy

World War II made of Osborn a Navy officer who won awards for his instructional air-safety cartoons that may have saved many lives aloft. But he emerged from it a caustic critic of Top Brass at work wherever you find it. Although "Proper Channels" (far right, opposite) could probably have been drawn only by one who himself had to go through them, its target, like that of the other drawings here, is universal: it could be anywhere.

"Incompetence"

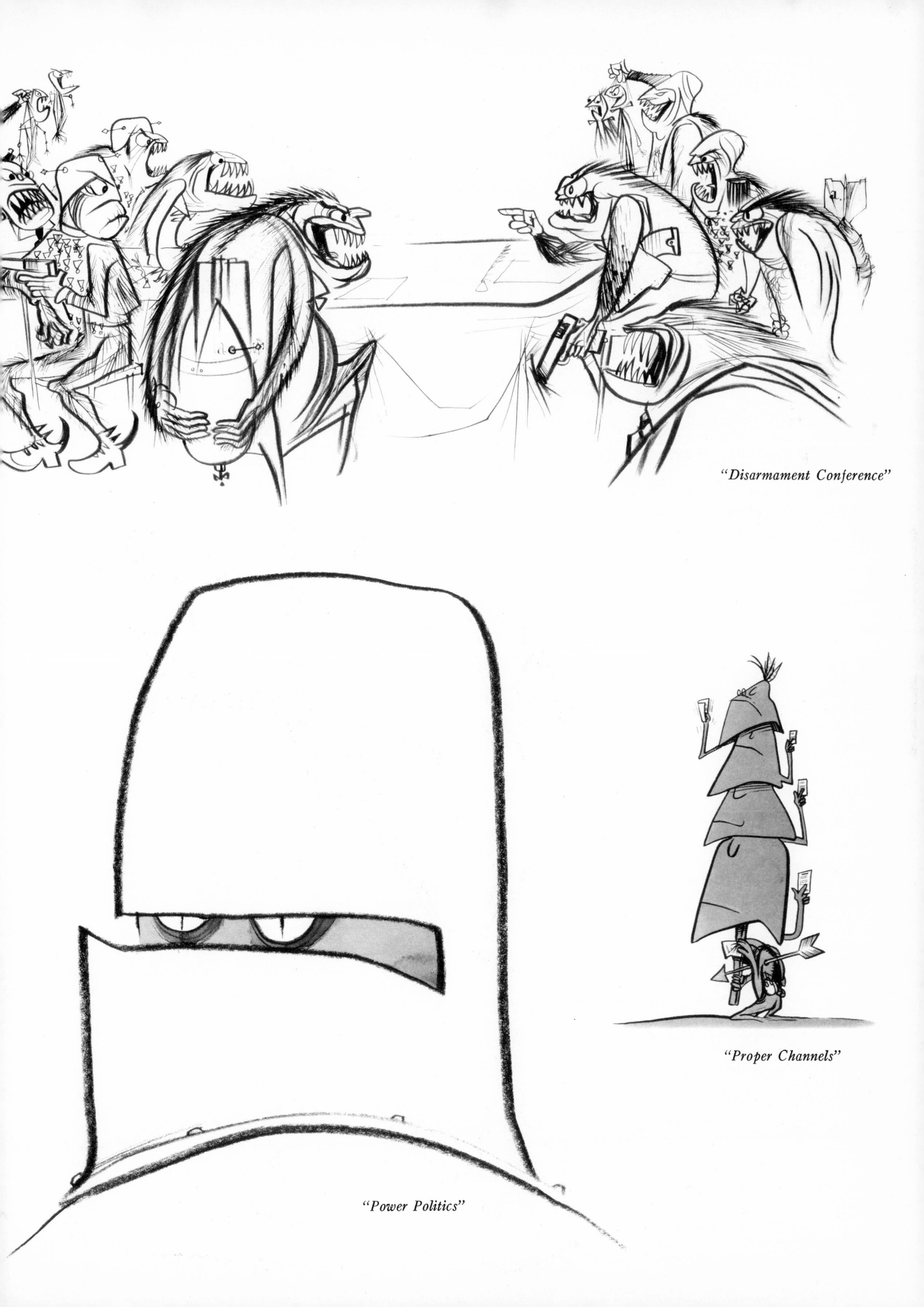

"Disarmament Conference"

"Proper Channels"

"Power Politics"

"Sex rears its ugly head . . ."

". . . and then YOU rear the family"

"In conceiving characters, the person I have in mind much of the time is myself," says the creator of Marty and many other figures esteemed in television, the movies, and the theater

AN INTERVIEW WITH PADDY CHAYEFSKY

By NORA SAYRE *and* ROBERT B. SILVERS

In the middle of the 1950's, during that brief period when television drama seemed more promising than it does now, Paddy Chayefsky became the best known of the small-screen writers. Realism flavored with Freud was his specialty: in most of his fifteen television plays, Jewish, Irish, or Italian working people used natural dialogue to express their thwarted emotions. Chayefsky's most popular television play was *Marty,* the story of a homely Bronx butcher who finally acquires a girl. After *Marty* was filmed in Hollywood, Chayefsky gradually withdrew from television to write for motion pictures and the theater. Another television play, *The Bachelor Party,* became his second film; *Middle of the Night,* the story of a garment manufacturer's affair with his secretary, appeared first on television, then on Broadway, and finally as a Hollywood production starring Fredric March and Kim Novak. Venturing into a writer-producer role, Chayefsky made *The Goddess,* a picture about a deteriorating movie queen, which was a commercial failure yet aroused much critical controversy. Last year he returned to Broadway as a playwright with *The Tenth Man,* which describes the encounter of a hallucinated girl and a suicidal young man in a synagogue, where old Jewish men are plotting the girl's salvation.

Small and stocky at thirty-seven, Chayefsky moves quickly and wastes no time on his entrances and exits. Tense but amiable, he professes to dislike interviews. However, he talks with gusto, his head thrown back, puffing cigarettes with the rhythm of his speech. Willing to take on any subject, he is ready with either anecdotes or panoramic judgments and inclined to weave backwards and sideways in recollection. Combative about his accomplishments, he also volunteers harsh criticisms of his own past work. Psychoanalysis has perhaps influenced his speech: his uninhibited monologues seem built on very free association.

In this interview, he repudiates many of his former views and announces a change in both the themes and the style of his work. Now impatient with the realism of *Marty,* Chayefsky's present ambition is a large-scale lyricism.

AN INTERVIEW WITH PADDY CHAYEFSKY

INTERVIEWER: An English critic recently wrote that "the pressure of commerce" made you leave television writing. Is that true?

CHAYEFSKY: It's thoroughly inaccurate. When I was growing up in TV, I used to argue for its advantages as a medium, but now I can't think of one reason in the whole wide world to write for a television program. Last year I said to Fred Coe, the producer, "Let's do another TV show together for laughs." But I welshed. I just don't want to write for TV.

INTERVIEWER: Why not?

CHAYEFSKY: Because I feel I would rather write plays for the theater. Any dramatic writer thinks of himself as a playwright essentially. If I have to make a second choice, it will be for a major film, even though films are *very* difficult to do well. The better screenplays are not necessarily good scripts or well written—they're often simply well stitched. You can't really *write* well any place but in the theater, as far as I'm concerned. You cannot write grandly. You cannot write with openness.

INTERVIEWER: How did you first become interested in writing?

CHAYEFSKY: I've been interested as long as I can remember. I was one of those editors of the high-school magazine and paper, that sort of thing, and I wrote some very high-schoolish stories, neo-Wodehouse, you know, with a touch of Dickens. I reread some of them with great embarrassment about three years ago. We had a very intellectual breed at De Witt Clinton High School—terribly precocious young chaps—and I hear from them occasionally. But I don't think it's good to be precocious in high school, because the very chaps who were aren't writing any more. One is in advertising, and he was a really brilliant boy, and another is anthologizing beat writers—a rather thankless sort of job, it seems to me.

INTERVIEWER: Did your teacher suggest that you might try to write professionally?

CHAYEFSKY: I did write short stories at City College where I studied with the late Professor Theodore Goodman, a very well-known short-story teacher at the time, but none of my teachers ever encouraged me professionally. I wanted to be a writer, you see, but I had no idea of how you go about being one—what application blank do you fill out? I squandered college, and I did rather badly. I'm sort of going back now on my own. I think people should go to college when they're about thirty-five and older—not any younger.

INTERVIEWER: Did your parents encourage you?

CHAYEFSKY: Oh, yes, indeed. I come from a standard Jewish family with standard Jewish values, and writers are highly-thought-of people among Jews. My mother is a very well-read lady, for an immigrant from the Ukraine. And my father, who was in the milk business and in building, was an absolute *aficionado* of the Yiddish theater. As a kid, I was a pianist. When I was five or six, I was giving cute little concerts in velvet suits at P.T.A. meetings. And to this day, one of the greatest joys I know is playing good music badly—I at least know how a *good* pianist would do it. And in a way, you know, it's the same with acting. I do a lot of bad acting-improvisation while I write. But I know what a good actor could do with the lines.

INTERVIEWER: Did you ever act?

CHAYEFSKY: Yes, in the Army, for a rather professionally done Army show which I wrote. And I did some night-club work, but I was very reluctant to perform.

INTERVIEWER: Was it in the Army that you did your first writing for the theater?

CHAYEFSKY: Yes, I was what you would call one of those bright young unknowns. While convalescing from a wound, in an Army hospital in Europe, I wrote a musical comedy called *No T.O. for Love,* which was produced in London under the auspices of a chap named Curt Conway. He directed the show and I played one of the leads. I must have ended up with ten years of theater experience from that one play. We toured Army camps and played in every conceivably and inconceivably difficult situation. And at the same time I slowly got to know some theater people in London: Garson Kanin, Marc Blitzstein, Laurence Olivier, Carol Reed, Claude Dauphin, Peter Ustinov—quite a group. They were all involved in a film called *The True Glory.* As far as I could see, I was the only combat-wounded man in the whole of London at that time—and the only one without paratroop boots, I might add. It seemed that all the paratroop combat boots had been saved for London personnel.

After the war I went back to New York to work in my uncle's printing shop, and Garson Kanin came along and gave me and some other chaps each $500 to write a play.

INTERVIEWER: Why did he do that?

CHAYEFSKY: Just out of friendship. No claim on it at all—not that I didn't wish he had. He was awfully helpful to me. I got to know a little group of veterans who wanted to work in the theater. I began to hang around the show-business bars in New York, and I tried to write.

INTERVIEWER: How did you go about starting that first play? Did you take certain playwrights as models?

CHAYEFSKY: Yes. I hadn't the slightest idea of how to write a legitimate play. After all, I had only written what might be called a "latrine" musical comedy, and then Curt Conway had sat over me and said "rewrite this—take that out," and so on. Well, when

---

This is another in HORIZON's interview series THE ARTIST SPEAKS FOR HIMSELF, under the editorship of George Plimpton.

I had my $500, I opened up my copy of Lillian Hellman's collected plays, because I remembered being so fetched with *The Children's Hour,* and I sat down and typed her play from beginning to end. *The Children's Hour* is a brilliantly put-together play, a masterpiece of architecture, and I set up my farce comedy on the same structure. It was called *Tentatively Untitled.*

INTERVIEWER: What was it about?

CHAYEFSKY: Needless to say, it was about a Jewish family in the Bronx. I was influenced by Clifford Odets as well as Lillian Hellman then. In fact, it would be difficult to find a writer of my generation, especially a New York writer, who doesn't owe his very breath—his entire attitude toward the theater—to Odets. Arthur Miller is an obvious example. The odd thing about Odets—I think he has yet to write his best plays. His last, *The Flowering Peach,* was quite a departure from his other things—you know, the old hard-bitten 1930 depression plays. Anyway, my own play was optioned endlessly, but nothing came of it, and I went on to write movie treatments and magazine stories for a while—none of which I sold.

INTERVIEWER: How did you come to try television?

CHAYEFSKY: I tried it because I was broke. When I got married in 1949, I was working as a gag writer for Robert Q. Lewis. Then he fired me on April Fool's Day—on the most amicable terms—but I didn't care because I'd just seen *Death of a Salesman* right after it opened, and that made me want to write a play for Broadway again. I called it *The Man Who Made the Mountains Shake,* and I wrote it for Elia Kazan. We worked on it for more than a year, but neither of us could finish it to his own satisfaction. My stamina was fine, but I just lost all interest and got into no end of fights with everyone connected with the play, and finally I just dropped it. I'd gotten flat broke in the course of following Gadg around, and he invited my wife and me out to Hollywood where he was doing *Viva Zapata!* So we went out there and stayed with the Kazans.

INTERVIEWER: Did you work on that film?

CHAYEFSKY: No. But, of course, I'd been out to Hollywood before—I first went out to study at the Actors' Lab on the GI Bill, and for a while I worked on film scripts. I know Hollywood very, *very* well. Anyway, when I got back to New York, I was quite broke, and Kazan got me a job writing radio plays, which I think is the most demeaning form of writing. But it's marvelous for your professional sense of humility. They don't need you—they just hire you. They paid $750 a script, and if you worked on it more than a week, you were a fool—the rewriting could run on for months. Finally I approached my friends in the theater—these included Sidney Lumet and Charlie Russell, who were director and producer, respectively, of a television show called "Danger"—and I wrote a TV play which Lumet directed.

INTERVIEWER: What sort of play was it?

CHAYEFSKY: It was a horror. I wrote it out of snobbery. I had a real look-down-the-nose attitude toward television, I must say. I needed money for rent and food and I received $700. The play was all about the assassination of a union leader in a phone booth. But I did try my best on my next script—for a show called "Manhunt." But neither of these shows came out the least bit the way I'd envisioned them.

INTERVIEWER: Why not?

CHAYEFSKY: Because I hadn't been present at rehearsals. In the instance of "Manhunt," they hadn't even told me that the show was in rehearsal. I made a vow I would never again do a show in which I wasn't in attendance at all the rehearsals. (I'm something of a nuisance at rehearsals.) Later, when I worked with Delbert Mann, who directed most of my best TV plays and movies, I would sometimes make hundreds of suggestions in a day, some good, many bad. It was up to him to pick and choose.

INTERVIEWER: What can a dramatic writer learn from television?

CHAYEFSKY: You learn your basics, and you learn them well. Most important, you acquire a professional attitude. There is no time for self-indulgence at all in television. You learn, for instance, how important the producer is: he's the brains of a TV show. He sets the tone, the caliber, the quality. He decides whether the script is good enough, and he picks the director. In fact, in any of the three dramatic media that I've been in, I'd say the producer is the most important man.

INTERVIEWER: How were your own producers?

CHAYEFSKY: I worked for Fred Coe, and—oh, my—what a fine producer he is! Coe got more freedom for the writer than most television producers, but he fought for every inch of it. His programs were a success, so he enjoyed the confidence of the networks and the advertising agencies. But I really don't know much about the back-door fighting in the TV world because when you worked with Fred you were never troubled by anyone—not the networks, not the agencies. If he said "Sounds like a good idea, go ahead and write it," that was the deal. I wrote about ten or eleven scripts for Fred. The third one was *Marty.*

INTERVIEWER: Those years between 1953 and 1955 are now thought of as the peak of television drama. At the time, were you conscious of being part of a particularly gifted group of writers?

CHAYEFSKY: Yes. It was a fascinating time. We all hung together in a creative *klatsch.* We were really intimate friends—Robert Alan Aurthur, Horton Foote, Tad Mosel, Dave Shaw, myself, and some others. We spent all day in Fred Coe's outer office or across the hall, up on the fourth floor at NBC. We were accused of all sorts of things—they called us the Diamond Typewriter Brigade. As a matter of fact, I got $1,200 for my five months' work on *Marty*—hardly the work of a diamond typewriter. There's an excitement about a genuinely creative Bohemia based on ideas and on contempt for money, and that was a febrile period which was marvelous.

One thing that most writers—and almost all writers' wives—forget: there is no such thing as a rich writer. A writer is a Bohemian, and he must always think of himself as such because he'll never be anything else. The writers who make many thousands on a movie should know it will never add up to the gay life of the very rich. Several of my friends have gone rather elegant. There's nothing wrong with the hoity-toity world: it is populated by people as charming as you'll find anywhere. But the writer himself is a man who works hard with his hands, who is an artist. If he forgets that, he loses his workmanlike integrity.

INTERVIEWER: Did you leave television to go directly into the theater?

CHAYEFSKY: No, I went out to Hollywood to make *Marty*—not because of "commercial pressures," as that English chap said, but because it was more exciting to make a movie—and as a matter of fact, I lost money doing it. I don't like Hollywood, but I love making pictures. However, it's not a fine writer's place. It's not a place for Arthur Miller or Tennessee Williams. It's certainly not a place for Thornton

Wilder. It's a photographic medium, a director's medium. I don't think that even in a pure art film the credit really belongs to the writer. Take the film *The 400 Blows.* It's a poorly written film, in the sense that the script alone would mean little to you. It's the directing—the conceptual work—that makes it an exquisite movie.

INTERVIEWER: Many of the other writers of your TV days seem to have gone on to Hollywood as well.

CHAYEFSKY: Yes, there has been very little evolution in TV, and many writers of my day have matured out of it.

INTERVIEWER: Do you think there is much hope for TV drama today?

CHAYEFSKY: I don't know what the possibilities of TV as a dramatic medium are. There are limitations imposed by the TV industry. I honestly never felt that I was under pressure myself, but certainly there are worthwhile plays that could not be done for TV because TV would not accept them. But then there are things you can't do in films, things you can't do on the stage; they are simply accepted as professional limitations. I don't know the answer to TV's problems. I do know that I don't enjoy watching TV. I watched it and identified with it completely when I wrote for it, but now, frankly, I don't remember the last time I sat down in front of my set.

INTERVIEWER: Do you feel you owe much to your television training?

CHAYEFSKY: A great deal. I spent ten very carefully calculated years of apprenticeship writing realistic TV scripts, and I gave myself a different craft problem in each one. I've been writing and learning like a professional student. Now I don't have to worry about whether the scene is set up right—my fingers can do the arpeggio without worrying about it. I wouldn't think of writing a western, say, or a story about the British army, because others could do it better. But I can put together a sensible script, a sequence of scenes (even in a western), as soundly, I think, as anybody in the wide world.

From here on in, it's the beauty of it that I'm after. After the years of writing realistic scripts for TV, I was finally able to give myself a delightful problem of craft in *The Tenth Man:* to marry off, to the audience's satisfaction, a lunatic and a suicidal maniac within five hours of their meeting each other. I suspect that's very much the way Shakespeare must have felt when he wrote *Richard III.* He must have said to himself, "How am I going to get Anne to accept Richard's proposal in a page and a half of dialogue?"

INTERVIEWER: Did you know the ending of *The Tenth Man* before you started to write the play?

CHAYEFSKY: Yes, indeed. That's just the kind of rule I've finally learned after ten years of work. I know what my ending is, and what it means, before I start my first draft. I may not know the exact course of events in the third act, or even all the events of the second act. But I will know *exactly* the last three minutes of the play, and I'll have written out notes on what the action is to mean to the audience. For example, even if I don't say they're going to get married in *The Tenth Man,* the action *means* they're going to get married.

INTERVIEWER: How do the ideas for a play first take form and how do you work them out?

CHAYEFSKY: Well, first I sit in my office in midtown New York—where I work from 10 to 5:30 every weekday—and scribble notes and ideas and possibilities on a pad. Then I may have to do considerable research. In the early days I wrote TV plays about the people I grew up with—the easiest people to write about—and the research wasn't elaborate. I worked in the

DRAWING OF MR. CHAYEFSKY BY GERRY GERSTEN

garment industry and the printing business, and my father was in the building business at one time; these are each the setting for one of my TV plays. One of the best television scripts I ever wrote was about a grandmother who insisted on looking for a job. The incidents are taken from the life of my own mother, who at the moment is seventy-five and working indestructibly away in a garment shop.

But to do *The Tenth Man,* I must have spent four months of the most enjoyable research, plunging into the mysticism of the Jewish religion. I have always been interested in the mystical and the unrealistic, and *The Tenth Man* was a simple statement affirming the satisfactions of the spirit. At any rate, one of the enjoyable things about being a writer is that you must read books. It's impossible to study the mysticism of the *Kabbala* without studying the medieval Catholic Church, and that led me into pagan rituals and the way they have been adapted into Christianity. By then I was caught in a fascinating search for beginnings, and that was one of the reasons I took my wife and kids to Israel last April. I took a movie camera, too, and I think I must have at home about forty-five minutes of the best footage ever shot of Israel.

INTERVIEWER: Do your ideas for a play change during the research period?

CHAYEFSKY: Yes, other people now contribute their feelings to the play, and I make changes in scenes all the time. In conceiving characters, the person I have in mind much of the time is myself—Marty is an example. I should think that every serious writer must give of himself up to a point, as an actor does. One of the things that amused me in college was the variety imputed to Shakespeare's characters. As you well know, you can take any of Shakespeare's women and transpose them into any other play. They are exactly alike. And Macbeth is Hamlet twenty years older, King Lear is Macbeth twenty years older; and the fact of the matter is, they are all Shakespeare.

I don't think variety of characterization was Shakespeare's forte. He was a very wise man—not too wise, sometimes not wise enough—but more than anything else, he was a great poet. Nobody has ever said the things he said so well.

INTERVIEWER: What happens when you complete your research and notes?

CHAYEFSKY: I type out a short summary of the play—a line of the main scenes from beginning to end. Your instinct comes into play here. You constantly ask yourself, "How can the action carry on from this point?" I work from this as I write the first draft. I finish each act carefully before I go on to the next.

INTERVIEWER: How many drafts do you write?

CHAYEFSKY: For *The Tenth Man* I did two drafts. When I complete a draft, I think I have a relatively finished piece of work.

INTERVIEWER: Have you always been able to arrive at the final form by the time you go into rehearsal?

CHAYEFSKY: Not at all. It took me ten years to learn to do it. Before *The Tenth Man,* I was always rewriting because the plays weren't properly constructed. The Broadway version of *Middle of the Night,* for instance, which was about a young girl involved with an older man who is her boss, was abysmally written—dreadful—and I never got it right until I rewrote it as a movie. I couldn't believe it had been a Broadway hit when I read it over, and I was forced to come around to the conclusion of most other people that it was really Edward G. Robinson, and not the play, that kept it going for two years.

INTERVIEWER: What particular things did you dislike in the play and how did you change them for the movie version?

CHAYEFSKY: Actually, there were so many faults I can only mention a few. First of all, it was neither the man's play nor the girl's play, and a play must be one or the other, no matter how many leading roles there are. In the movie there is no doubt that it is the man's story: it's his thinking, his progression, his decision that count, and the girl is in there only so long as she serves that purpose. I was surprised that Kim Novak took the part, frankly, because it was what I'd call a "featured" part, not a "star" part.

The play was much too clinical. And not believable. At the end of Act One, Edward G. Robinson takes the girl out to dinner, and when Act Two begins, it is several months later and she's fast in love. What the hell happened? In the film, the first stumbling months after the culmination of the affair are among the best moments of cinema I've seen. As Tyrone Guthrie said, it is a superb, unimportant picture—very competent, very professional and solid. It was a realistic show, the last of many I'd done, and I must say that I have no desire to write a realistic show again.

INTERVIEWER: You say your early plays were "realistic," but many of the plots end happily with love as the solution. Were you depicting life as you think it really is?

CHAYEFSKY: No, I think my endings were generally more hopeful than accurate. That is one of the problems of the realistic script—you can also describe it as a "No Third Act" script. There is simply no good solution dramatically for a realistic first and second act. For instance, *Raisin in the Sun* is an old-hat realistic play—if it had been about Jews, God knows, some people wouldn't have cared in the least about it. The charm of the play is in its absolutely lovely Negro characters. But there was no third act at all. I remember saying at the interval, "Watch out for the patchwork that's coming up now." With the possible exception of *Marty* and *The Big Deal,* my own endings were fanciful and tenuous.

INTERVIEWER: What else dissatisfied you about your own TV plays?

CHAYEFSKY: The restrictions on dialogue. In realistic plays like *Marty,* you cannot give the characters more skillful and better chiseled lines than they would naturally use. You have to keep chopping the impulse to write better, to make full use of the language. I like refined language, but it's impossible in a realistic play.

INTERVIEWER: Did your critics see that you were trying to shed realism when you wrote *The Tenth Man*?

CHAYEFSKY: Not all of them. The play was accused by some of being realistic, but it's not. It's a very stylized play, and it is directed in high style by Guthrie. It is, in fact, a throwback to the old stylized folk comedies of Europe. And I read considerable of the Weimar writers, Carl Zuckmayer, for example, and some old Yiddish plays, and I reread Molnár in order to get a proper feel for my play. Most of the criticism of *The Tenth Man* has hit at the ending. Some say they're sick and tired of all this love love love being the resolution to all the problems of current plays. Others ask how I could honestly recommend that a skeptical young man who is a suicidal maniac and a devout Jewish girl, a catatonic schizophrenic who seems possessed by evil spirits, go and get married, and how I could present this as a happy solution.

INTERVIEWER: What is your answer to these criticisms?

CHAYEFSKY: I guess there must be something unclear about the ending for so many intelligent people to feel this way. I think some people are confused by the last line of the play, a line that the producer Arthur Cantor, Tony Guthrie, and I wrote—*ensemble*—in a bar four days before we opened: "He doesn't believe in God, he simply wants to love," or something like that. We patched that line together because Guthrie didn't like the curtain line and had the charming idea of ending the show on a note of Talmudic disputation. But I would never recommend love as a solution—it is such a multi-meaninged word.

All I meant to say was that it is better to have faith in something—some form of dedication—than to believe in nothing, for belief in nothing is utter futility and endless despair. This young chap walks out of the play really believing the girl will become sane again, believing in the girl. I wasn't recommending belief in God or in dybbuks, for example, any more than I was recommending belief in Scotch whisky. I was just saying believe in anything, because it is belief which gives a purpose and a meaning and a sense of dedication to life.

And it seems to me that history bears me out. I've just finished reading *The Jewish War* by Josephus. What in heaven's name made those people, nearly a million of them, die in the siege of 69 to 70 A.D. over the question of Roman domination of their religion? Judea was an utterly sacked nation after 70 A.D. Yet you can't help but feel the strength and purpose in that belief: the Jews after all are still here—and where the hell are the Romans? And the Greeks and Assyrians for that matter?

The act of love itself—I think I say this in the play—is an act of faith, because you cannot measure, calculate, or define the feeling of love. And if you have faith in somebody, that's like saying you love them.

And if you want to argue on the realistic level, it is a fact that schizophrenics do function well if people around them have faith in them. As for the suicidal maniac, we all know that suicide is utter despair of life, but we can assume, for the moment, that this chap has no despair. So, even on the realistic level, it might work out. But in this play I was trying to describe in a symbolic way—given the present state of the American mind—the futility that always seems to follow periods of prosperity: the plunging after Billy Graham, the searching for togetherness, the whole religious revival, the desire for something to cling to, the utter meaninglessness of having achieved the wildest prosperity of all time and not feeling one whit the better for it, the sense of desperation and helplessness you can find in the work of so many writers. Well, I think we have been finding something to hold onto in the last few years, something quite extraordinary and not very different from the faith that I'm talking about in *The Tenth Man.*

INTERVIEWER: What is it?

CHAYEFSKY: I think we are finding a faith in our own genuine sensibilities. For the first time, by George, I think this nation of grocers, tradesmen, and philistines is becoming a nation of art collectors, gourmets, libertines, leisure lovers, and sensualists. They've found out about the individual's voluptuous reward—and historically it is a fact that in periods of national helplessness before great forces, people revert to the individual satisfactions of voluptuous and sensual things. I know little about the art of painting, but every time you turn a corner, somebody has just bought a painting. Why all this sudden interest in individual taste, in chic cars and clothes, in the arts, and in poetry?

Togetherness hasn't quite worked out. Let's face it. It was a feminine institution and men just couldn't fit into it comfortably. In the little world I live in, there has been a distinct reassertion of the male as master of the house, and so on.

INTERVIEWER: Do you think all this will affect the theater and the arts?

CHAYEFSKY: I think *they* must reflect the state of the times. Certainly some of my own plays of the middle fifties comprise the archetype of togetherness—especially the shrinking and incompetent men, as in *The Bachelor Party.* But there is, I think, a growing feeling in this country that a man is a man, a woman is a woman, pleasure is pleasure, sensual reaction is sensual reaction, and it is reaching the point of what I would call decadence. This is the soil out of which art grows.

INTERVIEWER: How do you explain the popularity of *The Tenth Man?*

CHAYEFSKY: I don't know. Everybody said I was an idiot to write it, and the day after the opening, the line stretched down to Eighth Avenue. I cannot imagine why people come to see *The Tenth Man.* It was meant to be amusing and not very profound; it was rather circumscribed in intent, and it's hardly the intellectual's meat, that is to say, it doesn't apotheosize Death. All philosophy can be boiled down to something awfully simple sooner or later. After I write a script, I go over it and cut all the "wisdom" out of it. And I don't know why people go to see specific plays. I can only tell you why *I* go to the theater.

INTERVIEWER: Why do you?

CHAYEFSKY: I personally enjoy stimulation, and, just as important, I would say, I want fun. I like to have a good time.

INTERVIEWER: I saw very little fun in your film called *The Goddess.* After all, it was the story of a successful actress falling to pieces. Were you satisfied with it?

CHAYEFSKY: Despite all the agony and trouble on that picture, and despite all the things that contributed to a very unhappy production—the only unhappy production I've ever had—the real trouble was the script. It was grim, clinical, and relentless. If I had patched it together before we went into production, instead of letting everybody tell me how marvelous it was, it would have been a successful script.

INTERVIEWER: What do you feel was wrong with it?

CHAYEFSKY: I was guilty of something I'm often wrongly accused of: psychoanalytical characterization. John Cromwell—the director—and I had intended in that picture to tell the story of the depression generation—we thought it would be a milestone among movies. But I never oriented the script properly. As the film stands, the explanation of the girl's life is too clinical.

INTERVIEWER: How do you feel about psychiatric explication as a device for the dramatist?

CHAYEFSKY: As a matter of fact, I made several cold-blooded, calculated attempts to solve a television drama by introducing a purely psychoanalytical motivation. One was a TV play called *The Sixth Year.* Kim Stanley was in it, and she was magnificent, and the play was a success; but it was one of the worst things I've ever done. I was looking for a way to resolve the realistic story, and I thought, "Maybe we can solve the emotional problem; that would be a decent dramatic resolution." But the aim of psychoanalysis, as I understand it, is not the least bit to make you solve problems or even to change or "adjust" but to make you enjoy what you are. I couldn't care less whether emotional problems are "solved." I find that some of the most neurotic, miserable, poorly married men I've met in my life are among the most fascinating and interesting people I know, as are confirmed bachelors, homosexuals, lechers of the worst sort who suffer the tortures of the damned. I enjoy these people more than any others. As for the women, the kookier they are, the more attractive they seem.

INTERVIEWER: Often you portray people whose main problem is their inability to love. You seldom deal with the problem of staying in love.

CHAYEFSKY: Listen, I'm bored with this love love love love love love thing, too! You know that I write so much of it. On the other hand, I'm bored with hate hate hate hate hate. The picture version of *Middle of the Night* had a nice clear statement. The play was a confused mess, but the picture was clear. It said that it is better to be unhappily in love, to be sickly in love, to be neurotic, diseased, gruesome, sordid, as long as it involves the passions of life. It is better to be all that than to be careful. It was better for the hero of that play to go into what may be the most heartbreaking experience that he knows, to suffer, to carry the torch, to find his wife sleeping in the park with another man, or whatever. It is better to suffer a genuine emotion and live than to be numb. But I do not recommend "love" as a solution.

INTERVIEWER: You do often concentrate on humiliation, don't you? For example, in three of your scripts—*Marty*, *Middle of the Night*, and *The Big Deal*—your heroes endure it. Why does humiliation so often attract you as a subject?

CHAYEFSKY: I hadn't thought about it, but, quite apparently, that kind of private pain strikes me as a fascinating dramatic thing to write about. I do find those things terribly painful myself. Sometimes I find myself dealing unpleasantly with people, talking to them as if they were animals, and I get physically sick. I just get sick, but it's the only way you get things done with some people. Yet I cannot bear to humiliate them, and I get twice as ogreish about it as I need be. Odd, it's the area of pain that I find interesting as a writer.

INTERVIEWER: Are actors sometimes overconscious of psychological subtleties in your work to the point of misinterpreting their roles?

CHAYEFSKY: Well, *Marty* is the obvious example. I did not intend to make it in the least psychoanalytic, although you could interpret it—if you happen to be a bore—as a study of latent homosexuality in the lower middle class, and so on. But that was not my intention. *Marty* was a comment on the social concept of what is attractive, of what constitutes love. The real problems of the script lay in the Mickey Spillane type of love and the egos of the people who were destroying the lovely moment Marty had. I remember Rod Steiger playing the part on television. He wanted to play his latent animosity to his mother and to all women in general. The director said: "Rod, play *love*. It's a love scene."

INTERVIEWER: Do you get on well with actors generally?

CHAYEFSKY: I like actors very much. I've only had two unpleasant experiences with actors. One with Kim Stanley, the other with Edward G. Robinson. I'm on very good terms now with Eddie, who is really an elegant man, and I think I'm on reasonably good terms with Kim, but it's hard to tell. She's an incredibly gifted actress, and the pain is worth it all. Aside from these two instances, I'm as vain as can be about my relations with actors. If they're improvising actors, I make no fuss about their cavalier attitude toward the script, but I ask the right to choose the part of their improvisation that stays in. In some parts of *The Goddess*, Kim rose to heights of improvisation, and, you know, much as I could have killed her, she had moments of magnificence. It was her script more than mine, believe me.

INTERVIEWER: What do you think of the technique of American actors?

CHAYEFSKY: You don't know how difficult it is to find American actors who can play style. To quote Guthrie, they pause so fluently. They pause and pause. With wit and charm you deliver a line, not a pause.

INTERVIEWER: Is this the Method's fault?

CHAYEFSKY: I do not like bad Method actors. With good Method actors, like Eli Wallach, you are unaware they're Method actors at all. But in the coming generation of playwrights, in the young talent emerging, I think you are going to find a lot of extravagant drama and verse—big romantic pieces. You must have actors of style to play them, and there are hardly enough now. American actors are as good as any in the world, but they're bound by the realistic theater.

INTERVIEWER: Do you think it would help if we developed a repertory theater?

CHAYEFSKY: I argue with Tony Guthrie about this all the time. Every time I see him he's on his way to start a repertory group. But such a group implies we have a theater and tradition of our own on which to draw, and we don't. We don't have any Shakespeare, any Racine—our tradition is O'Neill. We're not comfortable with the generic theater of other countries. To put it simply: we've had many performances of *Hamlet*, but somehow we feel it should be done by an Englishman.

At the moment I've got a Biblical epic in mind—it's to take place around 50 to 70 A.D., at the end of the sacrificial cult in Judaism—and, by George, I want to do it in style. I wonder if American actors will be accepted as Pharisees. I've always felt that a decent Biblical film should be done by Palestinians. They understand the language, the customs, the beliefs. Stephen Boyd's a very good actor in *Ben-Hur*, but we have no precedent for accepting him as a Roman, and Finlay Currie is not a Persian or an Alexandrian Jew, whichever it was Belshazzar was supposed to be.

INTERVIEWER: Who are some of the contemporary playwrights whose work requires the kind of style you're talking about?

CHAYEFSKY: Well, Edward Albee, who wrote *The Zoo Story*, and, of course, Ionesco and Beckett. And Williams has stayed alive with what Kazan calls the "to hell with it" kind of writing: "I don't care what you think, I like it, and to hell with it." And then Eugene O'Neill. He is so near the elemental instinct, right back to the Greek drama. He needs the brooding stylized performance of the Greek theater. Unfortunately, they play him realistically. I think we've seen the end, for the while, of the detailed realistic movement of which I was once in the forefront, I'm afraid.

INTERVIEWER: You feel that, with *The Tenth Man*, your work has changed tremendously, don't you?

CHAYEFSKY: Yes—thank heaven! I think *The Tenth Man* is the best thing I ever wrote. It is an orgasmic play. It's finished. It does its job. It's hard for me to find other things I've written that achieved this, with the possible exception of the film *Middle of the Night*. To me this means that I have finally found something I believe in enough to say, to hell with it—that's what my play means. My earlier work had insight but no passionate conviction about anything in it—clinical or ingenuously hopeful scripts. I daresay I don't expect to have that problem ever again.

Nora Sayre has served on The New Yorker *and has contributed to such other journals as* The Reporter *and* The New Statesman. *Robert B. Silvers is an editor of* Harper's Magazine *and* The Paris Review.

MUSEE CARNAVALET, PARIS

V. J. Nicolle (1754–1826): View of the Seine from the Louvre

THE LOUVRE

A crusading king began it. Brilliant successors enlarged it. Two Napoleons completed it. Sieges, uprisings, revolutions of taste have swept over it. First a fortress, then a palace, now Europe's greatest treasure house, this collective masterwork sums up seven centuries of French culture. Today it belongs to the world.

LOUVRE–GIRAUDON

THE LOUVRE

By ALLAN TEMKO

At sunset, an hour which is kind to the old monuments of France, the palace which by day is a shrine of democratic culture, the richest of museums, again asserts its royal splendor. For nearly half a mile along the Seine, the Louvre lifts its haughty roofs in the twilight to govern the center of the capital. The long façades, ornate with sculpture and classical orders, take the emerald light of the gardens, and gilt regal insignia glisten in the deep pediments. Unmistakably, the immense structure, reaching westward from the *vieux* Louvre of the Renaissance in two great arms that are themselves nearly five hundred yards long, is the work of kings. No royal residence in Europe—not even Versailles—is more vast and complex, and none is a more complete expression of a national past.

Like the slender river flowing past, bending out of the ancient core of Paris toward the broad city of modern times, the Louvre is an emblem of history. From the staunch medieval substructure of its oldest portions to the boldly romantic chimneys of the Second Empire, the palace sums up seven centuries of French civilization. No other building in the nation, not even the Cathedral rising a short distance upstream on its consecrated island, can do quite as much. For the Louvre, as architecture alone, spans the interval in time and space between the stone towers of Notre Dame and Eiffel's tower of steel, which is framed in the view westward across the Tuileries.

The vista extends through what is perhaps the most lordly display of controlled urban space in the world, in which the Eiffel Tower provides only a side note of emphasis. The main perspective extends down the central axis of the gardens, through the small Arc du Carrousel, across some fifty acres of *parterres* and formal lawn, down *allées* of chestnuts and linden, past the still lagoon, to the obelisk of the Place de la Concorde, and then up the long rise of the Champs Elysées to the Arc de Triomphe. As the evening deepens, and the great white arch is illuminated more than two miles away, the gardens in the foreground darken, the statuary turns to silhouettes, and the whole terrain of the Louvre can be imagined—as it was in the bright French dawn of the twelfth century—to be green fields.

The château was born with the Third Crusade. Significantly, it was the creation of a great king: Philip II, whom the Middle Ages called both "Augustus" and "the Conqueror"—with reason. During a forty-three-year reign that began in 1180, this shrewd and powerful Capetian drove the Plantagenets from Normandy and Anjou, fighting Richard the Lion-Hearted to a standstill and later routing John Lackland, so that England's continental holdings were reduced to a corner of southwestern France. He also exercised unprecedented control over his own nobles, who had often tyrannized his father, Louis VII, "the Young," and thus the feudal kingdom was decisively transformed into a centralized monarchy that led in time to the absolute state of Louis XIV.

Yet as Philip prepared to depart with Richard for the Holy Land in 1190 (Barbarossa had already left with a large army), he was uneasy. The Truce of God, he knew better than anyone, existed more in clerical theory than in medieval political reality. Richard might suddenly decide to abandon the Crusade—as Philip himself actually did—and return to invade his rival's territory. If not Richard, his erratic brother John might strike at Paris from the French-Norman frontier only fifty miles from Paris.

The capital was not even walled. Only the Ile de la Cité, on which the new cathedral was under construction, its nave still open on the west, was protected by an ancient rampart which dated from the first barbarian invasions. The royal palace, of which heavily restored portions remain in the present Palais de Justice, also stood on the island. Its towers and walls were part of the defense works, as were the crenelated palace and donjon of the bishop next to Notre Dame. These fortifications had not withstood the Norman pirates in the ninth century, and although they had been several times rebuilt and strengthened since, they no longer possessed real strategic value in a city which had burst out mightily from the insular confinement of the Dark Ages.

During the twelfth century, as life revived in France, Paris reflected the improving times and breasted out on either bank of the Seine. Population doubled and redoubled, so that it now stood at about 100,000. The semirural Left Bank, whose celebrated schools would soon be united under the charter of the University, was protected by three formidable walled abbeys. But the populous Right Bank, already the leading center of commerce and finance in France, and known as the Ville—"the Town"—to distinguish it from the island Cité, was virtually defenseless.

In a view from the left bank of the Seine, the fifteenth-century Louvre forms the background for the Retable du Parlement *by a Flemish master in which Louis IX is shown encountering John the Baptist. The royal residence must then have reached a peak of luxury, for in 1378 the Holy Roman Emperor on a tour was impressed by its wonderful walls and masonry, and a medieval chronicle relates that "through all the castle, as well as in the halls, the rooms, in the chapels, it was so prepared and arranged that nothing was missing."*

Philip ordered that it be enclosed with a prodigious semi-circular wall, surmounted by towers spaced roughly two hundred feet apart. Outside this wall on the west, in the open fields, where it could best resist an Anglo-Norman attack mounted up the valley of the Seine, he constructed the Louvre. Perhaps a hunting lodge, or *louveterie* (in late Latin: *lupara*), existed on the site and may have given the castle its mysterious and sonorous name.

This rugged bastion was never intended by Philip, or by any of the later Capets for that matter, to serve as a residence of state. Until the dynasty disintegrated in the fourteenth century, it clung atavistically to the venerable palace of the Cité which had housed the rulers of Gaul since Merovingian times. Philip's grandson, Louis IX—Saint Louis—constructed the Sainte-Chapelle in its court; and after 1300 Louis's grandson, Philip IV, continued to embellish the home of his ancestors, building the Conciergerie, where the cell which was to hold Marie Antoinette nearly five hundred years later may still be visited.

Under the Capets, the Louvre's main purpose was to serve as the key outer defense of Paris, and its unaffected military design plainly indicated its role. The burly walls formed a quadrangle seventy-five yards square, reinforced at each corner and at the center of each side by a massive tower and surrounded by a moat (see the historical ground plan on pages 82–83). The only entrance was between a pair of these towers on the east, facing a gate of the city and protected by a drawbridge and portcullis. Inside the walls, rising from a circular moat of its own, was a tremendous round tower—the *grosse tour*—one of the strongest donjons in Europe, its masonry thirteen feet thick at the base and rising above the surrounding walls to a height of 105 feet.

How quickly this fortress was completed is unknown. Perhaps the walls, which at first were only curtain structures with no rooms behind them, were finished when Philip returned from Palestine, prematurely bald and hardened by experience, only two years later. Almost certainly they were completed by 1200, when the city walls on the Right Bank were finished and the ten-year project of enclosing the Left Bank was undertaken. The Middle Ages built with more speed than is commonly thought.

In 1214, after his triumph at Bouvines, where he vanquished a coalition army led by the Holy Roman Emperor, Otto IV, and his own rebellious northern barons, Philip led back to the Louvre his most important prisoners, including Count Ferrand of Flanders, whom he kept in the tower for thirteen years. Throughout that century other feudal princes would come to the Louvre, either in chains or as chastened vassals, and yield to the Crown their ancestral lands and privileges. Gradually, as the military threat subsided, the function of the château widened: it became a real seat of government. Official acts were dated from the *"grosse tour du Louvre,"* which quickly became a symbol of the new strength of the monarch; and the royal archives, treasure, and collection of precious furnishings—the seeds of the future museum—were moved there for safekeeping.

But if the king governed from the Louvre, he rarely stayed in the apartments which apparently existed either in the tower or in a *corps de logis* built against one side of the quadrangle. Not only did the Capets prefer their more comfortable accommodations on the island, but the court still remained a traveling entourage, as it had been since barbarian days, moving from one establishment to another throughout the realm and enjoying periodic hospitality from vassals.

Nevertheless the interior of the Louvre gradually was filled with new structures. Saint Louis built a chapel within the enclosure, and against the west wall he erected a vaulted hall of justice where decisions modeled after Solomon's—unique in the Middle Ages for fairness and generosity, but occasionally marred by religious fanaticism—were handed down during a reign which in the history of the French monarchy was unequaled for its Christian idealism. It coincided with the completion of the great western façade and the transept roses of Notre Dame of Paris.

From this apogee, medieval civilization suddenly and tragically declined. As the Hundred Years' War erupted, and the Black Death swept over Europe in the middle of the fourteenth century, France entered a time of troubles. In 1356 the second Valois king, John II, was crushed near Poitiers by the Black Prince and taken to London as prisoner. Two years later the peasants of the Ile-de-France, exasperated by hardship and encouraged by the absence of the King, staged the violent uprising of the *jacquerie*. At the same time the populace of Paris, led by the provost, Etienne Marcel, rose in arms seeking a parliamentary regime. With unerring instinct one of their first moves was to occupy the Louvre. But these proto-democratic movements were suppressed as quickly as they had started. The authority of the Crown was re-established, fortunately not by a ruthless tyrant but by one of the ablest and most sympathetic figures of the late medieval world: the *"sage artiste"* Charles V.

His homely, intelligent face can be seen today in the medieval sculpture room of the Louvre: modest, almost diffident, his glance slightly averted, ready to break into a kind smile. As soon as he assumed power in 1364, surrounded by advisers who bore some resemblance to a modern cabinet, Charles undertook to transform the dour fortress of Philip Augustus into the home of a civilized prince. He enlisted one of the finest architects of the period, Raymond du Temple; and a fraternal architectural rivalry was conducted between the King and his brother, the Duc de Berry, who was building his sumptuous *hôtel* de Nesle just across the Seine.

From the duke's windows—as it appears in his famous

book of miniatures, the *Très Riches Heures* (page 63), and in other medieval illustrations—the new Louvre appeared as a palace of delight: a fairy castle of pearl-gray stone, studded with twelve tall towers (the great tower rising higher than the rest) surmounted by high, blue, pointed roofs, some round, some square, and capped with golden fleur-de-lis. Beneath this cluster of towers, the royal apartments and rooms of state had been refurbished and in parts entirely rebuilt; an upper story had been added and the walls raised some thirty feet, so that they were nearly twice as high as before. And although the walls were equipped with battlements and *poivrières* for archers, the structure had lost much of its forbidding opacity. Dozens of new rectangular windows appeared in the upper walls and gave a hint of what was to come in the Renaissance.

Moreover, there was a new sense of royal style, as well as a new-style king. Mounted pages carried golden dishes to his table in the banquet hall in the completely reconstructed northern wing, which was certainly the most palatial piece of architecture yet seen in France. Upward through its central tower spiraled the chief feature of the palace, a monumental staircase by Raymond du Temple, whose eighty-three broad steps twisted up through the construction like the ribs of a fan, each supporting the one above; it was a magnificent example of functionalist design, enriched by ten heroic statues of members of the royal family, leading to figures of the Blessed Virgin and John the Baptist at the top. In open niches between these statues were benches on which Charles loved to sit, speaking of his lions, which were kept in a menagerie in gardens which he himself laid out. They were not yet the *jardins à plaisance* of the Renaissance, although there were some lawns and fountains and flower beds, as well as open-air pavilions. The fresh mood of graciousness was enhanced by the library of nearly one thousand volumes in the north tower. Charles was the first important French bibliophile, and in certain volumes he signed his name under the phrase: "This book is mine."

The palace was at once pleasant and practical. Its military character, if softened, remained undisguised; and a new city wall, running northward from the river across the site of the present Arc du Carrousel, made it more formidable than before. For Paris had once again expanded with improving times. The nation's confidence had been restored; and by 1375, when the second Louvre stood complete, the army under Du Guesclin had surged back against the English, driving them from every part of France except a small pocket around Bordeaux. The future seemed bright.

Yet catastrophe followed, and gave Shakespeare material for his most patriotic history plays. "He'll make your Paris Louvre shake," thunders Exeter at the Dauphin in *Henry V*. The French disaster at Agincourt did more: it drove the monarchy from Paris itself—the tragic Paris of François Villon's childhood, when eighty thousand houses were abandoned, the populace lived on the verge of famine, and wolves entered the city. Even when the French returned, thanks to Joan of Arc, Paris frightened Charles VII. The seat of the Crown remained in the Loire Valley, and the Louvre was turned into a jail and an arsenal, a gloomy, neglected place in which fires could not be lighted lest the store of powder ignite.

Quite suddenly, to the rejoicing of the Parisians, the Court returned to the Louvre in 1527. Once again a new kind of sovereign occupied the throne: the greatest of the Valois, Francis I. Like Charles V a century and a half before, he was gifted, courteous, literate, and a friend of the arts—the man who brought Leonardo da Vinci to France. Unlike Charles, he was physically strong (a quality rare in this dynasty), sensual, and impulsive, but also shrewd to the point of cunning. The Clouet portrait in the Louvre (see page 70) shows a half-Italianized, extravagant prince of the Renaissance, his furred cap adorned with pearls and gems, his luxurious blouse of white silk embroidered with gold and richly striped with black, his manicured hand resting on a jeweled sword hilt.

He is a mixture of finesse and force. His elegant coiffure has been turned with an iron, but his neck is thick, his chin —beneath the rather unattractive beard—meaty, his nose exceptionally long and sharp, and his narrow eyes cold. He is the lighter French equivalent of Henry VIII, whom he met on the Field of the Cloth of Gold in 1520. At Pavia five years later, the astute Spanish Emperor Charles V led him captive to Madrid. In 1526, however, Francis was free and was again ruling France according to his *"bon plaisir."*

Immediately after his release, he announced his intention "henceforth to reside mainly in our good city of Paris . . . being aware that our castle of the Louvre is the most convenient and appropriate place for us to dwell; and for this reason we have decided to repair and put it in order."

His first step was to demolish the *grosse tour* of Philip Augustus. As the massive structure, nearly two hundred feet in circumference, came down, it must have seemed as if the last vestige of medieval government were being destroyed. Light flooded into the court of the Louvre.

Yet after this impressive beginning, Francis did relatively little more to the Louvre for nearly twenty years. In 1540, when he permitted Emperor Charles V to make an extraordinary military expedition across France to punish his rebellious subjects in the north, the Louvre was lavishly decorated for his reception. Yet even rich hangings could not hide the old castle's shabby and somber appearance—all the more somber in comparison with the resplendent new architecture that had appeared in the château of the Loire Valley, the gentle and gracious region where Francis was most at home. The new châteaux, built of the creamy stone of the Touraine, were white visions of a new humanism, scarcely fortified. They were meant for living, not for fighting, and stood as evidence of the nation's new internal security.

If France had rarely known peace during the preceding thirty or forty years, there had nevertheless been almost no fighting within its borders. From the reign of Charles VIII onward, the main contest with the Spanish enemy had been in Italy. Milan had become a French stronghold, and ambassadors, noblemen, prelates, bureaucrats, and soldiers—and above all architects such as Philibert de l'Orme, and writers such as his friend François Rabelais—crossed the Alps, traveling onward from Milan to Florence and Rome, where Michelangelo was at work. And not only Leonardo, but a number of other Italian architects, painters, and sculptors came to France, most of them renowned in their time and some celebrated still. Among them was Benvenuto Cellini, who arrived in 1540 after a characteristic act of violence caused him to flee Rome; his famous saltcellar, perhaps the ultimate expression of *arriviste* display, was made for Francis' table. Those notable Italians who did not come—Titian, for example, who painted the Louvre's portrait of Francis from a medal—nevertheless received generous French commissions. The royal collection, which was to form the nucleus of the museum of the Louvre, rapidly became one of the finest in Europe.

For the moment, most of these *objets d'art* remained at Fontainebleau, which had been only a hunting lodge at the start of Francis' reign but now became a veritable palace too. Between 1528 and 1540 the Louvre was forgotten while Fontainebleau was expanded and repaired. Classical decoration was used throughout, but the French medieval tradition of high roofs, chimneys, and fretted dormers remained strong in spite of Italian influence. A distinctly French classicism was being formed, and the Louvre in some ways was to be its most splendid expression.

Almost at the close of his reign, in 1546, Francis finally decided to make good his promise to rebuild the aged structure. For his architect he chose an *"homme nouveau"*: Pierre Lescot, who probably had not yet visited Italy but who, as an intimate of Ronsard, was in the forefront of the humanist movement. Rather than being a master builder in the medieval tradition, Lescot was one of the earliest of those amateurs of genius who in the next three centuries would design some of the finest buildings in Europe and America, including those by Thomas Jefferson. For although Lescot was paid well for his architectural work, he was first of all, like many outstanding Renaissance artists, a gentleman and a courtier. He was Lord of Clagny and Counselor to the King, and as Abbot of Clermont and Canon of Notre Dame of Paris, he also held Church benefices. Moreover, he had received an excellent education, studying not only architecture and painting but mathematics and the other liberal arts. He was probably in his late thirties when he commenced rebuilding the Louvre. Saint Louis's hall on the west side of the Cour Carrée was razed, and in its place Lescot created a masterpiece.

The façade, rising with exquisite grace to the low pitched roof, remains today much as it was built: a model of order and *mesure*. Three pavilions—at the center and on either side—project slightly and carry the eye deftly upward along pairs of fluted columns; the wall, growing richer as it ascends, breaks the horizontal moldings and the slender friezes of garlands and cupids, and stands free at last above the attic story in three beautifully drawn, curved pediments. The walls joining the pavilions are treated almost as richly. The rounded windows on the ground floor are set beneath finely modeled arches, but on the floor above, the windows are tall rectangles, capped with pediments that are alternately triangular and curved, and filled with carvings. In the attic, where mythological reliefs cover almost all of the wall surface, the windows are crowned with crossed torches. Separating the bays are fluted pilasters which carry the most ornate orders, Corinthian and Composite. They repeat the vertical movement of the half-columns of the pavilions, so that the façade everywhere flows upward with remarkable unity, its lines polished to subtle refinement, its carving gracious, all combining to give an impression of contained splendor.

It is a single vast relief, almost a painting in stone. The ornamental loveliness of the façade is scarcely related to the simple masonry structure behind it. Essentially the façade is a showpiece for sculpture, and what wins us—in spite of the fact that virtually all of the carvings were recut in the nineteenth century—is the perfect understanding between Lescot the architect and the sculptor who collaborated on all of his known work, Jean Goujon.

No elegance has ever been more French than Goujon's. Whatever influence Cellini may have had on him through works such as the *Nymph of Fontainebleau,* the Frenchman's lighter, elongated figures, enveloped in filmy drapery which falls about their slender limbs in intricate pleats, are completely his own. Like Lescot's architecture, which also is composed of classical motives developed in Italy, Goujon's sculpture shows French Renaissance art fully formed only a generation after its appearance on the Loire. How different the main directions of France and Italy were at this time can be seen in the powerful masculine cornice Michelangelo gave to the Farnese Palace, or in his later works, those impris-

Sowing their fields on the Seine's left bank with winter grain on an October day, fifteenth-century Paris peasants could watch the sun's glint on the blue towers of the Louvre beyond their city walls. In this miniature from the Très Riches Heures *of the Duc de Berry, the building is seen as expanded from the grim fortress built by Philip Augustus in 1190 into the exuberant château of Charles V almost two hundred years later. The central tower stood over the original donjon. Of this "old" Louvre, little now remains but foundations.*

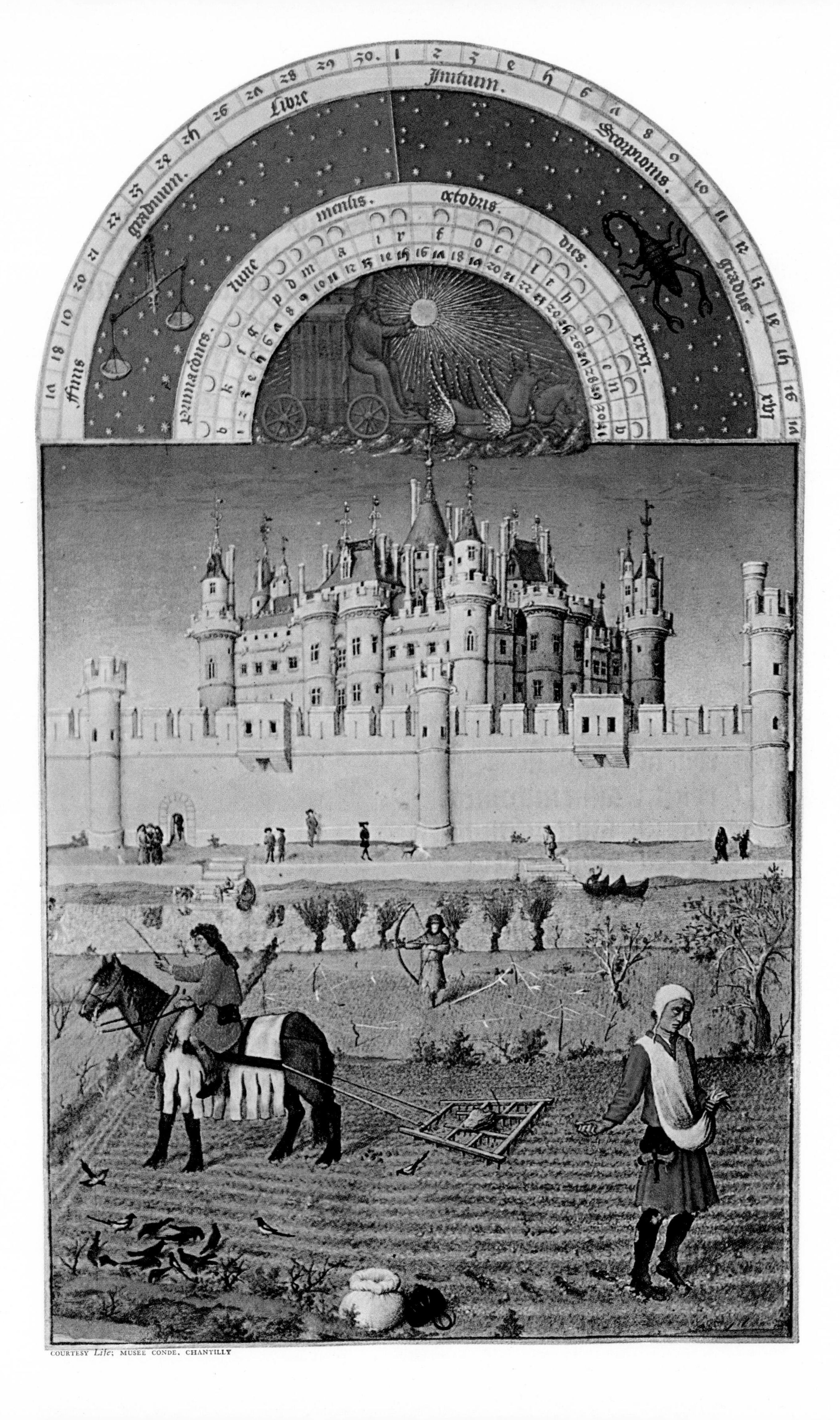

COURTESY *Life*; MUSEE CONDE, CHANTILLY

oned slaves who seem bound to the soul of the rock (see page 70), in contrast to Goujon's French ladies who seem to float on the surface of the stone.

The exquisite decoration of the façade was carried on within the Louvre throughout the 1550's. Because of vandalism and restoration by later ages, little of this work remains, but the vault of the staircase of King Francis' successor, Henry II, and the remarkable woodcarvings of Scibec de Carpi in the royal suite on the upper floor show how sumptuous it all was. And below is the completely restored Salle des Cariatides, the most famous room in the entire palace, in which four monumental female figures, inspired by those at the Erechtheum, support the tribune where musicians played while the dancers beneath, in costumes as rich as the plumage of birds, celebrated in 1558 the wedding of the Dauphin and Mary Queen of Scots.

The young prince, only fourteen, suddenly found himself on the throne when his father, the vigorous and cultivated Henry II, was struck in the eye at a tourney and died at forty. Henry's death ended the *ménage à trois* ambiguously commemorated in the royal monograms on the walls of the Louvre: an H interlocked with the double C of his queen, Catherine de Médicis—or was it not a D joined with the uprights of the H, and therefore the initial of Diane de Poitiers?

If ambiguity had existed, none remained now. It was Catherine's hour, perhaps the most evil and repulsive moment in the history of France. As her unfortunate sons, Francis II, Charles IX, and the degenerate Henry III, successively came to the throne, she and the Guises performed feats of treachery and cruelty, reaching an orgy of bloodshed on Saint Bartholomew's Day in 1572, that were unusual even in a cruel and treacherous age. The Louvre again became a battleground, and yet, whenever there was momentary quiet between Huguenots and Catholics, reconstruction of the palace continued.

If proof is needed that the Wars of Religion were politically motivated, the pagan Louvre of the sixteenth century offers evidence enough. Not a single Christian image ap-

MUSEE CARNAVALET, PARIS

The pageant of Paris in the 1650's was enacted daily on the Pont Neuf, where colorful throngs assembled to watch the royal coach and mounted courtiers pass to and from the new Louvre. To the right of the equestrian statue of Henry IV, the palace now combined that monarch's Grande Galerie (background), built at the turn of the century to give him a covered passageway to the new Tuileries palace to the west, and the even newer façade of the old court (foreground) designed by Le Vau, architect to young Louis XIV.

peared among the classical gods and goddesses, fauns and satyrs, nymphs and cherubs, which the sculptors continued to carve in the symbolic reliefs. The only iconographical subject was power, tinctured with carnality. The quality of the carving remained high, even though Goujon vanishes from history in 1563; possibly, some have claimed, he was a Protestant who no longer found his country safe and ended his days in Bologna. Lescot worked on, building the Pavillon du Roi along the river, with its tall roof, and then a south wing in the same style as his chef-d'oeuvre on the west. Probably he was in charge of the work until his death in 1578, thirty-two years after he first broke ground.

Yet after 1564 he had a great rival in the royal household. Philibert de l'Orme was the finest French architect of his time, who had built the wonderful château of Anet and then the magnificent bridge of Chenonceaux for Diane de Poitiers. After Henry II's death he fell from grace, but when Catherine decided to construct a palace for herself, outside the walls beyond the Louvre, on the site of an old tile factory—the Tuileries, she found she could not do without the master builder. De l'Orme, in contrast to Lescot, was a monumental rather than a decorative artist: he placed such emphasis on plain structure that he has been described as an "engineer." But he was far from that. He was, in fact, France's first modern professional architect, born in Lyons about 1510, the son of a master mason.

De l'Orme had his difficulties with Queen Catherine. His severe style, so much stronger than Lescot's, was too plain for her, and she badgered him to enrich the decoration of his monumental scheme for the Tuileries. All the details of de l'Orme's design are not known, but it seems certain that he envisaged an enormous rectangular structure, built around a vast central court and four smaller ones, with over-all dimensions of more than six hundred by two hundred feet. All that was ever undertaken was the long western façade, which in the course of time was so altered, before the Commune burned it in 1871, that de l'Orme's work was almost entirely lost. Yet before his death in 1570 he had at least

BIBLIOTHEQUE NATIONALE

Louis XIII, his mother Marie de Médicis (left), and his wife Anne of Austria, sit on a balcony of their new royal apartments in the Louvre's Petite Galerie; an engraving by Merian.

MUSEE CARNAVALET—BULLOZ

After the fall of the Bastille in 1789, Louis XVI returned from Versailles to Paris to try to stem the tide of revolt. In a painting by Houet, Louis and Marie Antoinette, sitting stiffly in their coach, pass the southeast façade of the

begun the domed central pavilion and completed its spectacular spiral staircase which appeared to be "planted in the air." Probably he also built the arcaded galleries which extended to either side.

With Lescot's wings of the Louvre, de l'Orme's nearby Tuileries provided the model for virtually all the work done on the palace in the following three centuries. In particular, his ornamental devices were imitated repeatedly, especially the "French order" which he added to the five classical orders of Greece and Rome. This was a column made up of superimposed drums in which the joints were encircled with decorative rings. The column was topped with an Ionic capital from which carven leaves and flowers, dear to French architects since the Middle Ages, grew downward over the fluted shaft.

With the beginning of the Tuileries, the royal family now had two tremendous establishments some fifteen hundred feet apart on the western edge of Paris, separated by the wall of Charles V and by a number of houses, shops, and churches —an entire *quartier*—that grew up between them. Both Lescot and Catherine de Médicis saw the possibility of a grand plan which would unite the two. The architect proposed to break down the remaining north and east wings of the medieval Louvre and to double the length of the new west and south façades, thus creating a new square court four times as large as its predecessor. The Queen, who perhaps had in mind the linking of the Pitti and Uffizi palaces in Florence, hit upon the idea of a great gallery along the river front which would connect the Louvre and the Tuileries. But the project was delayed as the Wars of Religion threw France into anarchy at the close of the century, and the Valois line vanished in tragedy.

The first Bourbon—the good-natured, reasonable, and brave Henry of Navarre, who entered the capital as a Catholic in 1594 because, as he is supposed to have said, "Paris is worth a mass"—took up the work with a will. Under two of the best architects of the time—Louis Métezeau working down-river from the Louvre, and Jacques Androuet du Cerceau the Younger upstream from the Tuileries, meeting where the city wall was breached—the Grande Galerie, the longest structure of its kind in the world, 1,374 feet long and about 100 wide, was erected between 1595 and 1610, although its interior was left unfinished (see air view of the Louvre as a whole, pages 84–85). The architecture maintained the mood of Lescot's Louvre, except that the pediments breaking the roof line were alternately round and triangular, rather than all round. Some ornamental details from the Tuileries also appeared; and in his portion, du Cerceau employed for the first time in a large French building the pilasters, ascending two full stories, that were popular in Italy. But these details only gave verve to the sweeping unity of the whole.

It was now clear that the Louvre was more than an immense work of architecture: the palace could already be recognized as the chief element of a new Paris which was gradually becoming the Western world's consummate triumph in urban design. The first royal squares—the Place des Vosges and the delightful three-sided Place Dauphine—were built at this time, as well as the Pont Neuf, completed in 1607. The bridge quickly brought about a transformation of the Left Bank, where the aristocratic *faubourg* of Saint-Germain now sprang up; and on the hill high above the river, Marie de Médicis constructed the Luxembourg Palace and its magnificent gardens.

Louvre as altered by Le Vau's successor, the architect Claude Perrault. As the spirit of the Revolution spread, the art collections accumulated over centuries by French kings were put on public view in the palace's new wings.

BIBLIOTHEQUE NATIONALE

Earlier, the trouble stirred up by Frondists, such as this agitator defaming Mazarin in 1649, moved Louis XIV to abandon the Louvre (background) for the pleasures of Versailles.

The Queen built her own residence because, when she arrived at the Louvre as a bride in 1601, she felt she had been brought to an uninhabitable palace. Whole suites of rooms were unfurnished; some were not even roofed. The north and east sides of the great court remained medieval. Nothing was accomplished during the minority of Louis XIII, the moody child who looked on unhappily as Queen Mother Marie, obese, coarse, and stupid, intrigued with the adventurer Concini and, as some said, became his "whore." In 1624, however, the masterful Cardinal Richelieu became chief minister to the Crown, instituting a regime of *Realpolitik*, and the King solemnly pledged that he would complete the palace of his ancestors.

Lescot's grand design for the Cour Carrée was finally carried out, even though neither Louis XIII nor Richelieu lived to see the work finished. The remaining medieval structures, including Raymond du Temple's staircase, were demolished, and the west and south façades were doubled in length, creating a space four times larger than the old court of the Middle Ages. Lescot's sixteenth-century elevations were faithfully duplicated for the sake of harmony; and in the center of the west wing, Jacques Lemercier's Pavillon de l'Horloge, with its colossal caryatids and ungainly square dome (pages 82–83), became the dominant feature of the ensemble.

The new scale was a measure of the increased strength of the monarchy, but the Crown still faced a last struggle with the aristocracy during the revolt of the Fronde, which Richelieu's successor, Cardinal Mazarin, crushed on behalf of the fifteen-year-old Louis XIV in 1653. But the outbreak had not been quelled in time to prevent the Parisian mob from breaking into the Louvre and demanding to see the child sovereign. The prideful, Spanish-born queen mother, Anne of Austria, who probably was secretly married to Mazarin, was compelled to admit a delegation to see Louis in his bed, where he pretended to be asleep. It was a portent of things to come.

The King, with smoldering rage, never forgot the incident. The end of the Louvre as the home of the monarch was decided that night: Louis was determined to live at Versailles, the country retreat where his father had found solace and which had already evolved from hunting lodge to small palace. But reconstruction of the Louvre continued nevertheless. Whether or not he lived in it, the palace had to remain worthy of so great a prince. Louis and his astute minister, Jean Baptiste Colbert, the *petit bourgeois* who paradoxically was the chief architect of the rigid social, economic, and political pyramid which culminated in the glittering person of the King, intended that the royal image, in Paris as elsewhere, should be overwhelming.

On the west, between the Louvre and the Tuileries, the wall of Charles V had already been razed, and a parade ground was created for such spectacular royal events as the display of horsemanship, or *carrousel,* held in honor of the birth of the Dauphin in 1662, which gave its name to the vast Place. Three sides of the Cour Carrée were now enclosed, although the exterior façades remained unfinished, awaiting completion of the east wing, where the full majesty of the King was to be displayed to the heart of the city.

The organizational genius of Colbert now took charge. Louis Le Vau, the chief architect of Versailles at this time, submitted a design for the east front, but Colbert was not satisfied and requested designs from other French archi-

MUSEE DE VERSAILLES

MUSEE DE VERSAILLES–GIRAUDON

Napoleon I brought fresh pomp and circumstance to the long-neglected Louvre, along with vast art treasures gathered as booty during his Italian campaigns. Above, in a painting by Serangeli, the Emperor during his coronation ceremonies in 1804 receives his army and civil chiefs flanked by Mameluke guards in the sculpture gallery of his new Musée Napoléon. As part of his spacious plans for beautifying Paris, he added a new palace wing along the Rue de Rivoli. The final master stroke was ordered by Napoleon III, shown seated (left) with the Empress Eugénie, in a painting done in 1853 by Tissier, studying the plans of Visconti to join the Louvre to the Tuileries palace.

tects. None seemed handsome enough. Colbert then approached four leading Italian architects, including Bernini, and in 1665 the master arrived from Rome to a princely welcome. Naturally his French rivals were irked, and Bernini's arrogance so infuriated them that his position was undermined. When he left for Italy that autumn, the foundation stone of the new façade had been laid, and it was understood that the structure would be built from his plans. His scheme called for a huge mass on the Roman order with colossal columns on both interior and outer façades, capped by a powerful cornice on which heroic statues were to be placed.

This grandiose design, which would have overpowered the rest of the palace, never rose from the foundations. Instead, Claude Perrault erected his famous Colonnade (see pages 66–67), which remains today the most distinguished portion of the Louvre.

Perrault was not a professional architect but a physician. In a sense, like Lescot before him, he was an amateur who was a favorite at Court. Yet he was versed in archaeology and possessed a remarkable command of the principles of classical architecture. Furthermore, as the concealed iron reinforcement and magnificent calibration of the Colonnade show, he was a superb structural engineer.

Rising on its unadorned, stately podium, which crosses the full 600-foot width of the façade, the rhythmical sweep of the giant paired columns—so slender for all their power, so vigorously yet gracefully organized beneath the low central pediment and in the pavilion at either end—reveals the architecture of the *Roi Soleil* at its highest moment. The grandeur and simplicity of the Colonnade were never equaled by later classical architecture in France, certainly not at Versailles. In Perrault's design there is clarity and sure strength, rather than theatrical pride. His classicism, like Racine's, is disciplined poetic emotion, calm—almost cold—in its symmetrical order, but charged with passion. Above all, it is a classicism that clings to humanism, even though the deification of Louis XIV is introduced in the Apollo theme of the decoration. At Versailles the King's pride was unchecked, and it was there that he finally took the Court in 1682.

Even though the *grand dessein* remained far from completion, all construction now ceased at the Louvre for over eighty years. The river façade of the south wing of the Cour Carrée was given a new front to harmonize with the Colonnade, yet other wings lay uncompleted and half-ruined with neglect. Some suites, such as the garish apartments of Anne of Austria, had been expensively decorated, but elsewhere the structure was still unroofed.

An ominous sadness hung over the unfinished palace, deserted by its royal occupant at the moment when, according to no less an authority than Christopher Wren, Paris had become a "School of Architecture, the best probably at this day in Europe." It had also become, as it remains, a unique school of urban design. Throughout the city, beautiful new spaces were created: the semicircular plaza before the crescent-shaped Collège des Quatre Nations (now the Institut de France) on the Left Bank directly across from the Louvre; the Court of Honor of the Invalides; the Place des Victoires; and the finest of the royal squares, the Place Vendôme. The greatest space of all was occupied by the garden of the Tuileries, extending westward from the palace toward the still pastoral Champs Elysées. The garden in 1661 had already "seem'd a Paradise" to John Evelyn, the English diarist. But three years later, André Le Nôtre completely redesigned its Renaissance outlines and created "a garden of intelligence." More human than the park of Versailles (though organized on the same premise of Cartesian geometry), it was enriched with embroidered symmetries of flowers, lawn, and groves of elm and beech and mulberry, with water playing at the end of the formal vistas.

The garden was open to the public (only liveried servants were excluded), and except for the unoccupied royal suites and the apartments in which a few important nobles continued to reside, the palace, too, could be freely entered by the people. Even in medieval times anyone could wander through the gates except when they were closed at night, and now those barriers were gone. The city of Paris, with all its energy, charm, disorder, and vice, literally crowded into the confines of the Louvre wherever there was room. A village of ramshackle structures had sprung up in the Cour Carrée; the Place du Carrousel would later be occupied by a *quartier* with its own streets and inner courts; the Colonnade was half-hidden by buildings jammed between it and the church of Saint-Germain-l'Auxerrois. The palace became a haunt of prostitutes, cutpurses, gamblers, and rakes. Just how public the Louvre was during the heyday of *ancien régime* absolutism could be appreciated in the corrridors and stairways reeking with filth, where aristocrats and commoners alike relieved themselves on the marble pavements.

Yet this was the palace in which, from 1659 onward, Molière's crystalline comedies were performed and where Lully's exquisite music was played. Here too, in 1672, was installed the Académie Française, which was soon joined by the Academies of Architecture and of Painting and Sculpture, and later by the Academy of Sciences and the Royal Society of Medicine. Long before the Revolution, the home of the king had been transformed into a home for the imagination and the intellect.

Indeed, hundreds of artists and artisans actually lived and worked in the studios on the lower floors of the Louvre's Grande Galerie, which had been opened to them in 1608 by Henry IV. Henry had intended these rent-free ateliers to become a "nursery of craftsmen, trained by good masters, some of whom would later be dispersed through the kingdom, and who would serve the country very well." His hopes were realized. Not only outstanding painters and sculptors but tapestry weavers, engravers, jewelers, and woodworkers as well enjoyed the hospitality of the Crown.

TEXT CONTINUED ON PAGE 72

TREASURES OF THE LOUVRE

Representing every age and culture, the vast collections of the Louvre include many of the best-known masterpieces in the history of art

This row from left to right:
De La Tour: "St. Joseph the Carpenter," detail, c. 1645
Tapestry, French, 16th c.
(Color) Egyptian sculpture, 12th Dynasty
Titian: "Man with Glove," c. 1523
Idol, Cycladic, 3000 B.C.
Stele, Egyptian, 19th Dynasty

This row from left to right:
Venus de Milo, Greek, 100 B.C.
Michelangelo: "Slave," c. 1513
Gericault: "Cavalry Charge"
Whistler: "Arrangement in Gray and Black," detail, 1872
Apollo from Paros, 6th c. B.C.
Ciborium, Limoges, 13th c.
Assyrian sculpture, 8th c. B.C.

This row from left to right:
"Marguerite of Provence," stone, French, 14th c.

Clouet: "Francis I," c. 1524

Cézanne: "The Blue Vase," c. 1890

Scribe, Egyptian, 5th Dynasty

Master of Moulins: "St. Madeleine and Donor," detail, c. 1490

(Color) Bust of a woman, wood and stucco, Italian, 15th c.

is row from left to right:

gres: "Self-portrait," 1804

olor) Christ of Lavaudieu, ood, French, 12th c.

antegna: "Calvary," entral portion, c. 1450

ust of Augustus, Roman

e Victory of Samothrace, reek, 4th c. B.C.

aumier: Drawing, c. 1868

This row from left to right:

Leonardo da Vinci: "Mona Lisa," detail, c. 1502

Plate, Hispano-Moresque, 15th c.

Agostino di Duccio: Virgin of Auvillers, detail, 15th c.

Rembrandt, "Self-portrait," 1660

Bell idol, Greek, c. 700 B.C.

Ivory, detail, Byzantine, 5th c.

Leonardo da Vinci: "The Virgin of the Rocks,"detail, 1599

COLOR TRANSPARENCIES: REALITES–*Les Merveilles du Louvre*

TEXT CONTINUED FROM PAGE 69

Still, it was the artists and intellectuals who led the outcry in the middle of the eighteenth century against the long neglect of the palace. Voltaire, typically, protested in verse against the *débris honteux* which littered the deteriorating structure. In 1755 the Marquis de Marigny—who, thanks to his sister Madame de Pompadour, had been named Director of Royal Buildings—started work on the Louvre once more. Although he engaged architects of the stature of Jacques Ange Gabriel, creator of the Place de la Concorde, and Jacques Germain Soufflot, who was later to design the Pantheon, there was no question of carrying the *grand dessein* further. Limited funds enabled Marigny only to clear the Cour Carrée and the Colonnade of the old buildings that blocked them; to roof the north wing and level the dome and roofs that spoiled the river façade on the south; and to refurbish parts of the interior, although the Grande Galerie and other important halls remained sadly dilapidated. In 1774 construction ceased again.

Nevertheless the intelligentsia, with Diderot and other Encyclopedists as their chief spokesmen, continued to urge that the Louvre should not only be repaired and completed but also transformed into a great museum. The idea was not new. As early as 1679 a *cabinet des tableaux du Roi* had been opened to the public; so, soon after, were the annual expositions of the Academy of Painting and Sculpture.

But these innovations had done little to make the riches of the royal collections available to the people. With the departure of the Court from Paris, the Louvre had lost many of its finest works to Versailles where, an angry critic charged in 1747, they were "buried in badly lit little rooms" and virtually unknown "because of their inaccessibility." Marigny set up a temporary museum in the Luxembourg, where Parisians could examine more than one hundred paintings by Leonardo, Raphael, Veronese, Correggio, Titian, Rembrandt, and other masters in the royal collection, but this provided only a tantalizing glimpse of the treasures which the public was now convinced it had the right to enjoy. Paris was already the center of the art world. Its galleries and auctions were famous; and collectors, who were called *curieux*, came from as far as Russia to make purchases.

The Comte d'Angiviller, an ambitious collector for himself and for the Crown, succeeded Marigny in 1774 and immediately set out to make the museum a reality by starting to convert the Grande Galerie into a true exhibition space, fireproofing the construction and planning to open skylights overhead. But time was running out for the Old Order. Perhaps if a monarch of the stature of Henry IV had been on the throne (and present in Paris) the enterprise could have been carried out; but the King was Louis XVI, and he remained at Versailles, uncomprehending and weak, until the royal family reluctantly returned to the Tuileries on October 6, 1789. Three years later, on August 10, 1792, the mob surged into the palace. But by then the King had already bungled his attempt to escape, and the guillotine had been in operation for five months on the Place du Carrousel. For the execution of the King of France the following January, the machine was moved to the Place de la Revolution—no longer a Place Royale and not yet the Place de la Concorde.

While these cruelties were taking place, and the young Republic was fighting for survival, the National Convention did not forget the museum. On August 10, 1793, the Grande Galerie was opened, and not only were masterpieces of the old Louvre collection shown but also new "precious spoils taken from our tyrants, or from other enemies of our country." Throughout France churches were emptied of works of art, such as Jan van Eyck's *Madonna of Chancellor Rolin* (taken from the Cathedral of Autun). The residences of noblemen were ransacked: two of Michelangelo's sculptures of slaves, for example, were found in the Paris town house of the Duc de Richelieu. Some of these works were placed in storage, some went to provincial museums, but the majority of famous masterpieces eventually came to the exhibition rooms of the Louvre.

Then, as Bonaparte advanced through Italy, the museum's collection of both antique and Renaissance art was expanded almost beyond belief. Under the terms of armistices and treaties, thousands of pieces were selected by French experts from the galleries of Parma, Modena, Milan, Bologna, Perugia, and, above all, Rome and Venice, and then transported triumphantly to Paris. When Bonaparte moved on to Egypt,

TEXT CONTINUED ON PAGE 81

LADIES of the LOUVRE

Of the 200,000 works of art (including 5,000 paintings) housed in Europe's greatest museum, none lend it more color, grace, and impact than the paintings of women—chiefly Frenchwomen—by Frenchmen. Of these, HORIZON *presents on the following eight pages a selection in color gravure. A world of difference separates Ingres's classically poised portrait of Mademoiselle Rivière (opposite) from Fragonard's playful exuberance, Manet's once-scandalous boldness, Degas's psychological insight, Renoir's and Seurat's delight in sheer atmosphere and light (exemplified on subsequent pages), but a Gallic warmth of feeling unites them all.*

INGRES: "MADEMOISELLE RIVIERE," 1805

ENCICLO
PEDIE
TOM
IV
TOM III

FRAGONARD: "THE BATHERS"

QUENTIN DE LA TOUR: "MADAME POMPADOUR," 1755

(OVERLEAF) MANET: "OLYMPIA," 1863

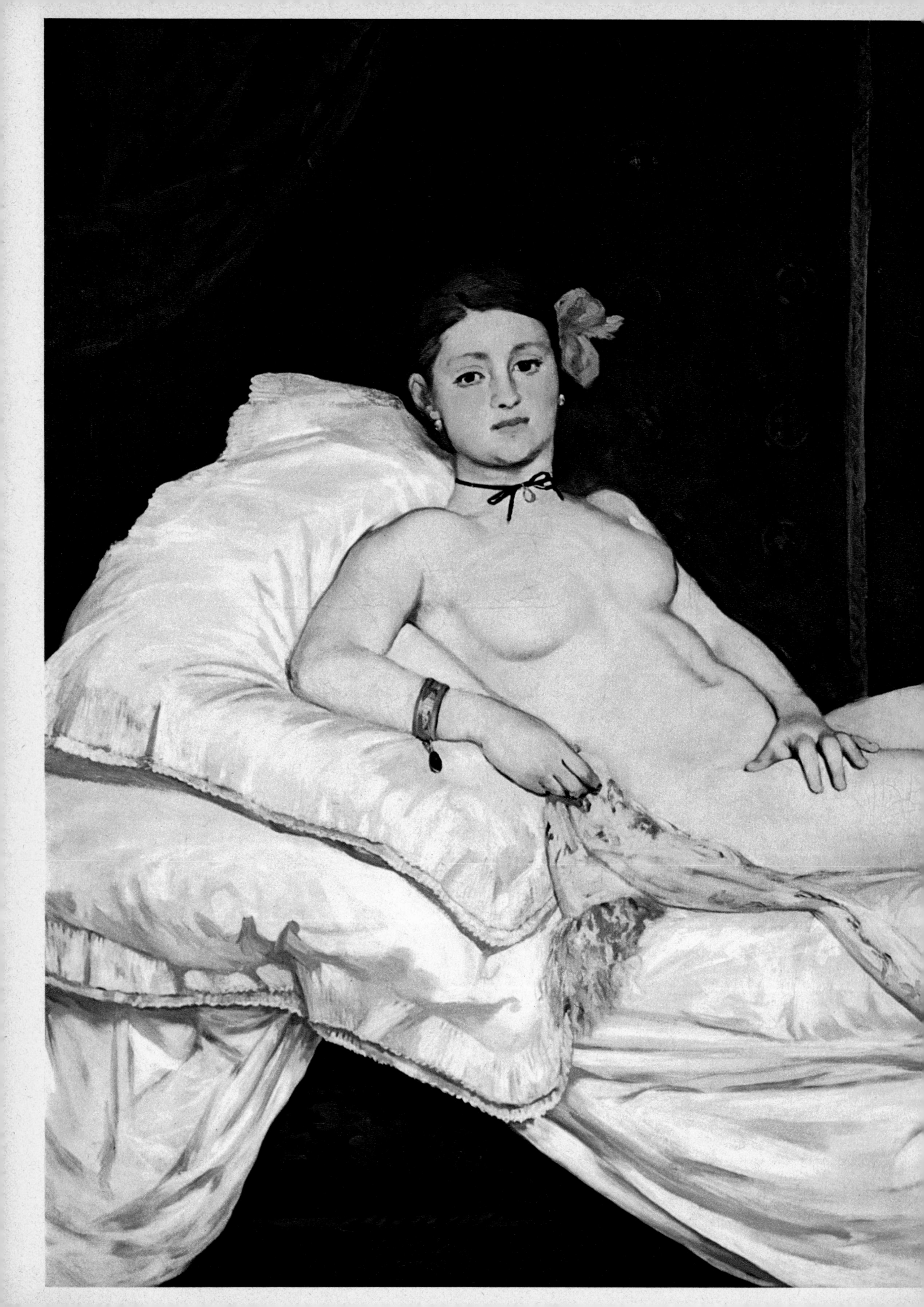

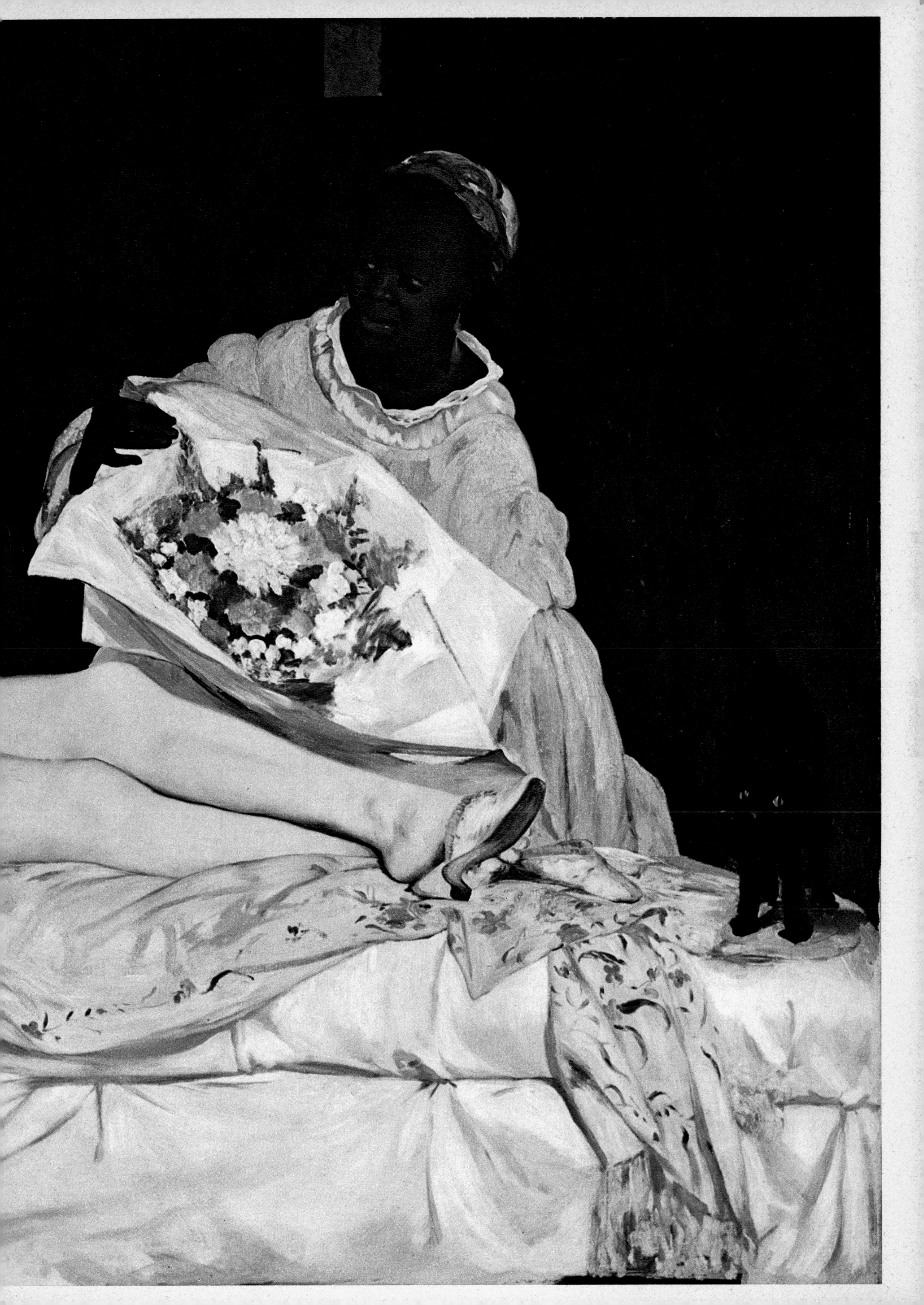

Degas

RENOIR: "THE SWING," 1876

DEGAS: "ABSINTHE," 1876

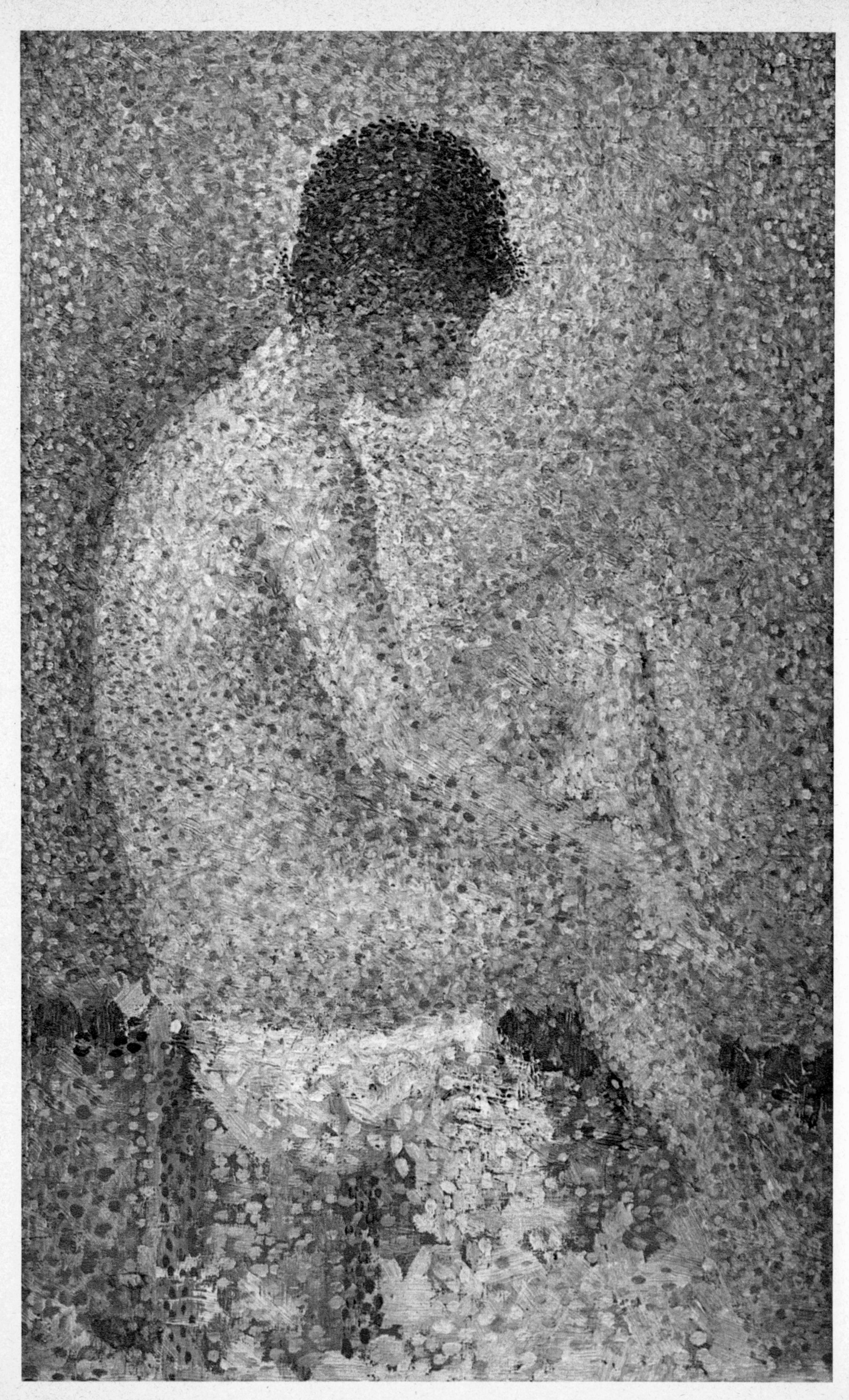

SEURAT: "MODEL IN PROFILE," 1887

TEXT CONTINUED FROM PAGE 72

a stream of Middle Eastern antiquities also commenced to pour into the Louvre.

Comparatively little of this artistic loot was ever returned, and to accommodate it all, as well as to make the palace a residence worthy of his imperial person, Napoleon revived the *grand dessein* with the vigor and boldness characteristic of all his undertakings. The Emperor was the first to grasp the possibilities of the palace as the central element of a sweeping new city plan for Paris. As whole blocks of ancient buildings were destroyed and the splendid arcades of the Rue de Rivoli replaced them, as the Rue Castiglione was cut through from the Place Vendôme to the Tuileries gardens, the Emperor's architects, Percier and Fontaine, embarked on a program of construction such as had not been seen at the Louvre since the days of Perrault and Le Vau.

The Cour Carrée was finally completed; the Grande Galerie was extensively renovated; a group of magnificent monumental staircases, ascending two and three stories, embellished the Louvre and the Tuileries; and on the north side of the Place du Carrousel, a second great gallery, foreseen for centuries, was begun between the Tuileries and the Louvre. This tremendous wing, its design inspired by the handsome river façade of the Grande Galerie, does not run exactly parallel to the latter, for the older structure diverges perceptibly from the central axis of the palace. Therefore the northern gallery also slants inward as it approaches the Louvre. The irregularity is considerable, but the vastness of the Place overcomes it: in fact, the lack of exact symmetry gives the composition an extra baroque verve, springing the great intervening space into motion, which a stricter formula would not have done.

Waterloo prevented the Emperor from completing the *grand dessein.* A large gap remained on the north when the Empire collapsed, and the famous horses of San Marco—which Napoleon had placed atop a fussy little arch of triumph which Percier and Fontaine erected in the Place du Carrousel—were returned to Venice. Yet Napoleon had unique fortune among dictators. The middle-class kings who succeeded him carried on his projects as best they could despite the tidal force of revolution which surged into the palace in 1830 and again in 1848, when the Tuileries were pillaged and the Louvre invaded and momentarily threatened with destruction. The Second Republic was determined to make the vast royal establishment a *palais du peuple* for once and all, but the Republic was betrayed once again by a Bonaparte, and the *grand dessein* was completed in the name of the Second Empire three full centuries after it was launched by Lescot.

The new Louvre of Napoleon III has only recently been appreciated as one of the extraordinary architectural achievements of the last century. Whatever the failings of the architects Visconti and Lefuel, however ruthless their demolition and total reconstruction of a full half of the Grande Galerie, however banal the neo-Renaissance ornamentation which replaced the sensitive reliefs of the sixteenth and early seventeenth centuries, the new Louvre has a richness and a gusto which make it one of the great works of romantic architecture. The remarkable three-dimensionality of the pavilions, the bold fantasy of the tall chimneys and roofs, the wild massing of the sculptural groups on the high pediments and dormers which seem almost to fly out of the structure below, actually do not represent slavish eclecticism but prodigious originality.

If the new Louvre is *parvenu,* like the regime which in just five years between 1852 and 1857 accomplished what previous governments could not do in three hundred, its coarseness vanishes before the magnitude and uninhibited quality of the work. The new Louvre is not a palace; it is a romantic vision of a palace, meant for every possible public use except as a permanent home for a hereditary dynasty.

The regime of Napoleon III, like its predecessors, disappeared in violence. Yet in 1870, when the Empress Eugénie fled terror-stricken from the Tuileries, through the Grande Galerie and the *vieux* Louvre, to hail a cab half a mile away in front of the Colonnade, she drove into hiding through a Paris which her husband, now a prisoner of the Prussians, and Baron Haussmann had utterly transformed. It was the Paris of the tree-lined boulevards which remains the most handsome and pleasant of all great cities, in which large public monuments are set as jewels—in the neutral context of the long, gray avenues.

Haussmann had designed these thoroughfares for the purpose of controlling the people. Never again, he hoped, would the barricades appear in the twisting medieval streets of Paris, where artillery could not be brought against them and the populace could rise up with the figure of Liberty at their head, as in Delacroix's painting in the Louvre. But during the Commune of 1871—the short-lived insurgent government which Marx perhaps mistakenly saw as the first real example of proletarian rule—the people again stormed out of the ancient quarters and attacked the home of the sovereign. On the night of May 23–24, the Tuileries burned.

If the architectural loss was great (although certainly not so great as fervent French antiquarians maintain), the liberation of urban space was an immeasurable gain. As the ruins were demolished, the tremendous vista opened, giving the center of the city its exhilarating sense of civilized freedom, surrounded but not confined by the past. The palace, with all its treasures, continues to serve the complex modern state as a hive of government offices in the wings which front on the Rue de Rivoli. And through the gardens, as the tourist buses arrive at the Place du Carrousel in the morning sunlight, stroll the people not only of France but of the world, to whom the Louvre belongs.

Allan Temko, who often contributes to HORIZON *on present-day architecture, is the author of* Notre-Dame of Paris, *as well as of a study of Arles in the July, 1959, issue.*

OVERLEAF: THE LOUVRE THEN AND NOW

A BUILDING GROWS OVER SEVEN CENTURIES

A unique product of as many hands as generations, the Louvre began as the long-since demolished fortress and château of medieval Philip Augustus and Charles V, the outlines of which (including the circular central tower and dungeon) are shown in this historical plan as situated in what later became the easterly Cour du Vieux Louvre, or Old Court. Anchored to this origin, the Louvre then radiated in all directions, with a mighty surge to the west along the Seine's banks in Henry IV's Grande Galerie (shown in ochre). Poorly related at the time to the Louvre, Catherine de Médicis's Tuileries (gray, near left) next went up, leaving an indiscriminate clutter of buildings in between. Finally, under Napoleon I and III, the problem of linking the two was solved, and the great cleared, enclosed space around the Arc du Carrousel (left center) was created. Following the Tuileries' burning in 1871, the Third Republic retouched the edifice and gave it the final imprint we know today.

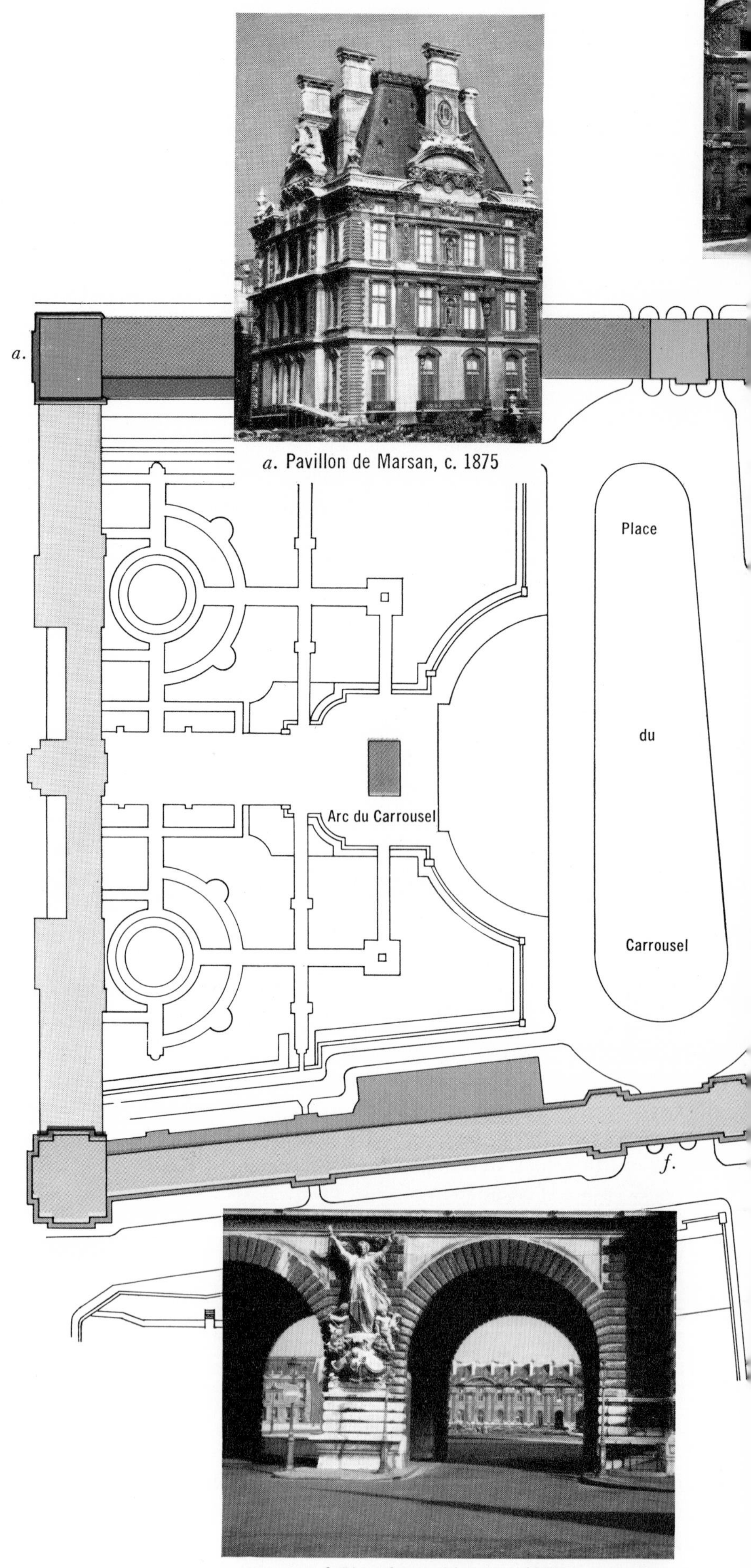

a. Pavillon de Marsan, c. 1875

f. River-front archway, c. 1870

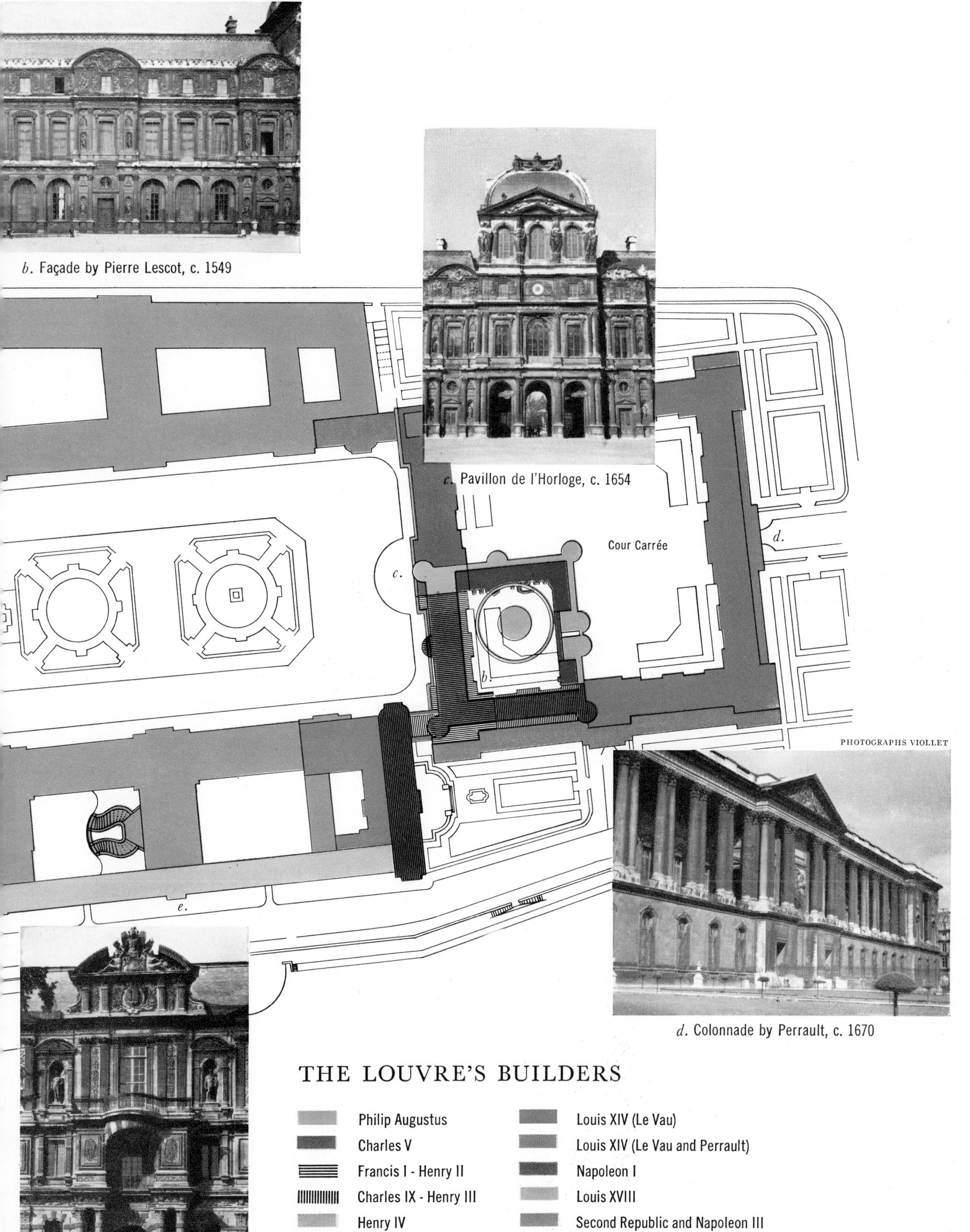

GIRAUDON

b. Façade by Pierre Lescot, c. 1549

c. Pavillon de l'Horloge, c. 1654

PHOTOGRAPHS VIOLLET

d. Colonnade by Perrault, c. 1670

e. Porte Barbet de Jouy, c. 1608

THE LOUVRE'S BUILDERS

- Philip Augustus
- Charles V
- Francis I - Henry II
- Charles IX - Henry III
- Henry IV
- Louis XIII
- Louis XIV (Le Vau)
- Louis XIV (Le Vau and Perrault)
- Napoleon I
- Louis XVIII
- Second Republic and Napoleon III
- Third Republic
- The Tuileries—built for Catherine de Médicis, destroyed in 1871

OVERLEAF: An air view presents the Louvre today with the Tuileries garden in the foreground.

PHOTOGRAPH CHARLES ROTKIN

DESIGN BY JOEL SZASZ

COME AGAIN

On Stage: RICK BESOYAN

Little Mary Sunshine is an off-Broadway musical comedy of undeviatingly innocent worldliness—very like a Baker Electric with wicker coachwork in a drag race—that has played to capacity audiences since it opened last November. About as fruitful a clue as may be found to its longevity and the frame of mind of its composer, author, lyricist, book director, co-arranger of the vocals, and properties chief—a short, dark, round-faced, muscular man of thirty-six named Rick Besoyan—is contained in his prefatory note to the script. "It is absolutely essential to the success of the musical," reads Besoyan's adjuration, "that it should be played with the most warmhearted earnestness. There should be no exaggeration in costume, make-up, or demeanor; and the characters, one and all, should appear to believe, throughout, in the perfect sincerity of their words and actions."

The fact is that Besoyan himself is perfectly convinced of the sincerity of his words and actions. These days he is an earnest practitioner of Zen (as well as a wholehearted lifter of bar bells), the principles of which, Besoyan lately realized, he had been applying even before he had learned them formally. He summed these up as: "The bottom turns into the top and the top turns into the bottom; I mean you can be the most funny by being the most serious." Thus *Little Mary Sunshine* is seen at once to be not so much a satire on the sentimentalities of its antecedents—the operettas of Victor Herbert, Rudolf Friml, and Sigmund Romberg—as an exegesis of their absurdities. What Besoyan has done, if his notion of Zen is right, is to make people laugh by gravely standing them on their heads.

The fine foolish plot of *Little Mary Sunshine* bears the greatest resemblance to Friml's *Rose Marie.* The Northwest Mounted Police have been transformed, disarmingly, into Forest Rangers. (Their tunics are still a blazing red, however, and their teeth, frequently exposed, give the eerie impression of being the best money can buy.) Their mission is to capture a treacherous Indian holed up in the brush somewhere in the neighborhood of Little Mary's debt-ridden hotel in Colorado. Everything, of course, turns out fine: the mortgage is eventually burned; Little Mary and Captain "Big Jim" Warington reach their glutinous heart's desire; the Indian is not merely captured, he is rehabilitated; and for every ranger there is a visiting Eastern society girl.

Besoyan has, in one way or another, been a professional in the theater for a dozen years and, before that, an amateur from the age of nine, when his father bought him a two-dollar ukulele with instruction book included. (The year after that, it was a guitar; and the year after *that,* ten lessons on a piano rented for ten dollars for ten weeks. Besoyan again studied piano, in London, while still in the Army, then worked with the American Theatre Wing, and after that became a voice teacher when he wasn't behind the soda fountain at a Schrafft's restaurant in Greenwich Village.)

In a way, *Little Mary Sunshine* is the outgrowth of economic and cultural accidents. The Besoyan household prospered until the Great Depression. It had a windup Victrola and piles of selections from, among others, *The Red Mill, Naughty Marietta, The Firefly, The Vagabond King, Rose Marie, Maytime, Blossom Time, The Student Prince,* and *The Desert Song.* After 1929 hard times set in; no more records were bought and young Besoyan was happily reduced to playing the same things over and over again. It was years before the primitive boy discovered Cole Porter, George Gershwin, and Irving Berlin. He was, however, exposed to a school production of *The Mikado.* Nothing in his experience of American operetta having prepared him for the phenomenon, Besoyan was thoroughly shaken to find that not only was the music "pretty" but that the libretto and lyrics were "funny" at the same time. He was subsequently entranced by the realization that all three were of a piece.

Besoyan's relationship with *The Mikado* and his apprenticeship in the theater were both long. Before settling permanently in New York, he played Ko-Ko in the Savoy Light Opera Company production of *The Mikado* some five hundred times throughout the United States and Canada, to say nothing of roles in the operettas with which he grew up. *Little Mary Sunshine* was written, revised, and polished over a three-year period. A truncated version was put on in a Greenwich Village night club a few years ago. It then took Besoyan nine months, more than fifty auditions, and 127 investors to raise the $15,000 needed to put it on.

It is no coincidence that Besoyan has half a dozen program credits, right down to "properties man." His preoccupation with the synthesis of all the elements of a production (not excluding himself) is extraordinary and possibly touching. "As yet," he said, "it's an insoluble problem. *Oklahoma!* and *The King and I* come closest. I don't mean to be presumptuous with my elders and betters, but the thing that interests me, the solution I'm trying to find, is how to unify book, music, and lyrics perfectly." He peered anxiously into some distant future in which, presumably, he would write, compose, direct, and produce. "I'm loaded," he said, "with ideas. Three specifically. I'd rather not say what." He squared his shoulders manfully. "I'm going right on with this program of unified musical theater. The mission will take me the rest of my life."

GILBERT MILLSTEIN

Photograph by EUGENE COOK

On Screen: LEE REMICK

With the luxuriant improbability that has always characterized Hollywood affairs, Lee Remick has successively been cast as an Arkansas child-bride–drum-majorette, a Faulknerian baggage stirring up lust in Mississippi, a dance-hall hostess, the not-unhappy victim of rape, and a wild hoyden (resident on an island in ole Tennessee) who blooms with sensual yearnings for a T.V.A. agent. In all of the five films in which she has appeared, she has been required to comport herself as a girl of somewhat easy ways—if not quite a tart, then an *enfant sexuelle* with swivel hips and parted lips. The composite image formed by her roles is to Miss Remick as the image in a funny mirror of a carnival side show is to a giggling but otherwise normal girl who confronts it: wickedly distorted yet intriguing. For the actress is a young lady born in Boston and reared with all propriety. And not since Katharine Hepburn sloped out of Hartford, Connecticut, has the Yankee gentry—or the *haut monde* anywhere—yielded to the theater or the screen a talent of like mettle or flexibility.

Finished at Miss Hewitt's (her father a department-store owner, her mother a beauty and an actress of accomplishment), Lee Remick at twenty-four, tawny blonde, shapely as a drawn bow, conveys the same sense of inbuilt tension with the promise of sudden release. Distinctive and quite herself, she is becoming recognized as an actress of particular promise and already sizable achievement, at once animally magnetic and genteel.

Lee Remick was never urged toward the theater, although when she was twelve years old she did read Shakespeare for six months with the British coach Isobel Merson. She studied dancing until she was eighteen, practicing the art in summer stock and traveling in the choruses of several musical-comedy road companies. But for the most part, her background was that appropriate to a proper Bostonian.

After entering Barnard College in New York, she became a frequent performer on television (agents had already noticed her when she was briefly brought to Broadway at sixteen by Reginald Denham for a leading role in *Be Your Age,* a dismal juvenile comedy that withered quickly). Before completing a semester, however, Miss Remick abandoned college. "I'm horribly educated," she remarks. She did not next enter the Actors' Studio, the temple and training ground of so many of Elia Kazan's chosen Method players. Asked why not, she replies: "People say that you'll lose whatever it is that makes you different. And to get up in front of twenty-five people to be picked to pieces—it would almost ruin me. Once I did take a whack at studying drama, in Mary Welch's workshop. I gave up right away, couldn't stand the scrutiny. I was like one of those flowers you touch and they close right up."

Lee Remick's conversation is candid and gusty (occasionally underlined by the sudden direct glances of the clear blue eyes—of a hue generally to be observed in Western sheriffs). She recounts how in May, 1956, she appeared in a television drama in which she portrayed a young girl from Pennsylvania who goes on a mad fling in Nassau. The critics were impressed, as was Kazan, who asked her to audition for a role in the Budd Schulberg movie *A Face in the Crowd.* "I got the part," she recalls. "I played a drum-majorette in a contest judged by Lonesome Rhodes, the hillbilly singing idol. I give him the business and wind up as a fifteen-year-old bride in a New York penthouse with my own soda fountain. It was a small part, but a good one; being directed by Gadg made all the difference."

The next year she obtained a contract with Twentieth Century-Fox with options to do outside work. She has played in two films for Fox: *The Long, Hot Summer,* from William Faulkner's stories, a *succès d'estime* directed by Martin Ritt, one of Broadway's ablest men, and *These Thousand Hills,* a tone poem to the West exhibited briefly and best forgotten. "They conned me into that one," she says; "I know enough now to hold out for what is best for me."

It was in Otto Preminger's independent production of *Anatomy of a Murder* in 1959 that Miss Remick made her most notable mark. As the victim of a rape which triggers a murder and the principal witness at the subsequent trial, she was exact and startling. With her oscillating gait, the actress employed her sly touch in small matters. To a tawdry role she brought inherent grace and marshaled a calm delivery with a change of pace worthy of Satchel Paige: her slow stare alternately titillating and alarming the defense attorney (James Stewart), her demure parries deflecting the rattlesnake thrusts of the prosecutor (George C. Scott).

Last spring Elia Kazan once more directed Miss Remick in a characteristic performance of passion and restraint in *Wild River,* a sometimes rough, sometimes tender story of an old woman and her untamed granddaughter defending their ramshackle home against the encroaching commonweal of the T.V.A. Inquiry about that assignment provokes a mock groan from her. "We nearly froze in that river in midwinter. God, how I want to play in a summer picture—one in which I'm a rich girl with fancy clothes, just once."

In her next picture, Miss Remick is fated to enjoy only part of her wish. Although the climate will be hot, she will be seen against a seamy background stitched together from Faulkner's novel *Sanctuary* and his play *Requiem for a Nun.* Miss Remick will be Temple Drake, the much tarnished heroine, this time the victim of ravishment, an addict of drugs—indeed, the archetypal southern Gothic cathedral of female ruin. But at least—and at last—she will play a well-born wanton.

ROBERT EMMETT GINNA

Photograph by SAM SHAW

WINES
STOP

By WALTER TERRY

DENMARK'S ROYAL BALLET

The Kingdom of Denmark is not very large and, by contemporary standards, not a world power. But four million Danes are not at all upset by this state of affairs. They have charm (irresistible to tourists) and they have pride. They are proud of the success of one of the most complete welfare states in the world; they are proud that their king, Frederik IX, represents the oldest monarchy on the European continent; they are proud of their heroic past—at one time they conquered practically everything in sight; and they are enormously proud of their ballet, which is a direct link between that past and the present.

The Royal Danish Ballet, currently on its second tour of America, boasts a tradition stretching back to the establishment of the Royal Theater in Copenhagen in 1748—some thirty-five years before the building of the Bolshoi Theater in St. Petersburg, home of the Imperial Ballet. The Russians, however, with considerable justification, point out that *they* had an Imperial Ballet School as far back as 1738. The Danes coolly counter this claim by reminding everyone that a full-scale Danish court ballet was performed as early as 1634.

But age alone is not the key to the Danes' unique position in the international world of ballet. For one thing, the Danes are bent on preservation. Ballets created more than a century ago are still performed in Denmark almost exactly as they were at their premières. This is possible only because the Royal Danish Ballet, despite the addition of new creations to the repertory, has kept its great classics on the stage year after year. No other company has done the same. With others in Europe and America, traditional works have been subject to continual restagings and rearrangings. As a result, we can only guess what the original *Giselle* of 1841 was like, or even the much later *Swan Lake,* which is now performed in innumerable versions around the world.

In addition, the Danes possess a very special category of ballet masterpieces that belong to no one else. These are the works of the great ballet master August Bournon-

ville (1805–1879), who also established in Denmark a style of dancing that is now known simply as "Bournonville." Both the ballets and the style have been preserved by generations of Danish dancers who follow a curriculum cannily devised by the old master to keep his work alive. The classroom exercises taught daily at the Royal Ballet School are composed of movements and combinations of steps extracted from the original Bournonville ballets. One day the techniques will be derived from *La Sylphide,* another day from *Napoli,* and so on throughout the week.

The distinctive Bournonville style is best described, perhaps, in his own words about himself: "I danced with a manly *joie de vivre,* and my sense of humor and my energy have always made an impression in every theater. I seemed to make the audience happy, and before they admired me they liked me." The Bournonville qualities of energy and humor—and, in the male dancers, of manliness—characterize the Royal Danes to this day.

Other personal traits became, during the fifty years of Bournonville's administration, part of the Danish ballet tradition. As a dancer he always had difficulty with turns ("I have worked hard to surmount . . . a swaying of the head in the pirouettes"), and so there are not many elaborate turns in Bournonville ballets. A virile personality himself, he choreographed skillfully and generously for male dancers. Thus, in Denmark, the male never experienced the abject decline in prestige that overtook other male dancers with the coming of the Romantic age and its single-minded exploitation of the ballerina—a state that persisted until the flashing arrival of Nijinsky.

Bournonville, in fact, brought to Denmark the fruits of two balletic eras. Following his own early studies in Copenhagen with his father, Antoine, who was then the Danish ballet master, he journeyed to Paris to study with the celebrated Auguste Vestris, one of the last great figures of the pre-Romantic ballet. But he was also in Paris when the Romantic age was born: when themes changed from the myths of ancient Greece and Rome to the later European legends of sylphs, wilis, and other supernatural creatures; when the ballerina, rising onto her toes for the first time, became the desirable but infinitely elusive female; when Marie Taglioni formally ushered in the age with the immortal ballet *La Sylphide* (not to be confused with the later *Les Sylphides,* by Fokine, which was inspired by it).

In 1836, four years after Taglioni appeared in *La Sylphide* in Paris, Bournonville staged his own version—with a Danish score and with the Danish ballerina Lucile Grahn in the title part—in Copenhagen. Although retired, half-forgotten, and, on occasion, halfheartedly revived by other companies, *La Sylphide* never left the repertory of the Royal Danish Ballet. Through this and other Bournonville creations, we can still see the first flowering of the Romantic ballet as it really was—a world of ethereal maidens floating through the moonlight into the arms of their spectral lovers. And through *The Whims of Cupid and the Ballet Master,* the oldest ballet extant (created in 1786 by Vincenzo Galeotti, Bournonville's illustrious predecessor at the Royal Theater), we know something of the style and form of the pre-Romantic ballet, especially its comedy idiom.

The particular treasure of the Royal Danish Ballet may well be Bournonville, but the Danes are not content with the conservation of relics. In the 1920's Michel Fokine restaged three of his finest works for the Danes: *Les Sylphides, Petrouchka,* and *Prince Igor.* With their customary exactitude the Danes have preserved them just as Fokine staged them. Several ballets by George Balanchine, Jerome Robbins's rollicking *Fanfare,* and the magnificent evening-long *Romeo and Juliet* (created especially for the Danes by England's Frederick Ashton) have become part of an impressive repertory that also includes such classics as *Giselle* and *Coppélia,* as well as ballets on Danish themes by Danish choreographers.

In the Royal Ballet School, where carefully selected children start a lifetime of training at seven, the Danes keep pace with the times. In addition to the traditional Bournonville classes, which give the Danish dancers their fabulous leaps and jumps, the Russian-born Vera Volkova teaches the most advanced ballet technique—the dazzling turns and complex point-work demanded by contemporary choreographers. Through her own coaching genius—she numbers England's Margot Fonteyn, America's Maria Tallchief, and Denmark's own Erik Bruhn among her pupils—she has succeeded in fusing the Danes' native exuberance and innocent candor with the sophisticated elegance and grandeur of the Russian ballet tradition.

In the past, Denmark has shared with the world such individual artists as Lucile Grahn, an honored colleague (and rival) of Taglioni; Adeline Genée, who became the toast of London and New York; Paul Haakon, a headliner in American musicals and on the concert stage; and, most recently, Erik Bruhn, one of the really great *premiers danseurs* of our era. But not until recently has it shared the whole of the Royal Danish Ballet with audiences in other lands. Now that the company itself is traveling, the American public is not simply tasting a piece of Danish pastry in the form of the talents of one dancer but, rather, savoring a rich Danish *smørrebrød* of the dance, seasoned with rare Galeotti, vintage Bournonville, and other artistic flavors created by the Danes during the course of two remarkable centuries of Royal Danish Ballet.

Walter Terry is the dance critic of the New York Herald Tribune. *His most recent book is* Ballet: A New Guide to the Liveliest Art.

Right: Although he now dances with other companies as well, it was in the Royal Danish Ballet that Erik Bruhn acquired his great strength and flawless line. Preceding pages: In The Whims of Cupid, *oldest surviving ballet, it is one of Cupid's whims to blindfold pairs of lovers—Blackamoors, classical Greeks, Quakers, etc.—mix them up, and let nature take its course.*

© EZRA STOLLER

FRANK LLOYD WRIGHT'S WAR ON THE FINE ARTS

A foe of the academicians of his youth, he later grew to disdain painting and sculpture generally and to see architecture as the only art. End result: a museum that defeats the works it houses

By JAMES MARSTON FITCH

He died just short of his ninetieth birthday and just before the opening of what he surely considered to be one of his major works. For Frank Lloyd Wright, the Guggenheim Museum in New York would have been important not so much for its size or complexity but because it represented his final conquest of a lifelong adversary—the metropolitan East. Death robbed him of this sweetest victory; but even in death Wright remains the focus of controversy. Everyone has been forced to comment on the museum and no one has found it possible to be neutral. On only one point does there seem to be agreement: that however handsome it is as an architectural fact, it is not successful as a museum.

Seen from the outside, the great exploding spiral is a powerful landmark; within, it appears as a magnificent vessel for containing the crowds, displaying them to far greater advantage than does the dress circle at La Scala or the grand staircase of the Paris Opéra. But it does not display painting or sculpture to equal advantage. On the contrary, with perverse if not malicious skill, Wright's museum dwarfs the art it might have been expected to magnify. He has set the individual pieces afloat in a vortex, a whirlpool, an interior volume of absolutely overpowering movement. He has taken unfair advantage of the artists: of poor dead Kandinsky, with his intersecting circles and delicate pastels; of elegant, modest Brancusi; of gay Miró. He has reduced them all to the level of lonely little shepherd boys, piping away in competition with *Lohengrin.* Michelangelo himself would be unsafe in Wright's museum.

The realization of his failure must come as a disappointment to the admirers of Frank Lloyd Wright, but it should not come as a surprise. The museum is merely a statement, in reinforced concrete, of his lifelong conception of the relative importance of architecture and the fine arts. For him, architecture was always literally "the mother of the arts," absolute in its supremacy over all the others. In the last decades of his life it became more and more the *only* art. No other architect of comparable stature has minimized art as consistently as he. Little mural painting or sculpture appears

GEORGE CSERNA

The great spiraling ramp of Wright's Guggenheim Museum is a better setting for the crowds than for the paintings.

P. E. GUERRERO

as an integral part of his later work. In those buildings over whose interior design he exercised control, there is not only little contemporary Western art, there is not even a place for it—physically or aesthetically. Nor did he ever, in these latter decades, give any evidence that he could collaborate with independent artists, as did the elder Saarinen with Carl Milles or Niemeyer with the muralist Portinari.

And yet Wright was not always able or willing to exclude art from his life or his buildings. On the contrary, there was a time in his early manhood when the problem of the fine arts and their relation to architecture occupied much of his attention. During the first two decades of his practice, he wrote and spoke extensively on the subject and worked closely with a number of artists and craftsmen. Many of his houses employed sculpture and painting in a wide range of media—fresco, tesserae, stained glass, cast concrete, wrought iron. And he began, during just this period, that collection of Oriental prints which was to make him one of the greatest collectors in the nation. What, then, is the origin of his later attitude toward art—especially modern Western art—that mixture of hostility to, contempt for, and bland ignorance of the work of his contemporaries in the fields of painting and sculpture?

In 1887, when Wright arrived in Chicago as a fastidious, arrogant, but very perceptive young man, he looked at the middle-western art world and found it worthy of nothing but hostility and contempt. It is unfortunate, both for Wright and for art, that this initial exposure led to prejudices that were never to change. But if we follow him closely during those critical years from 1887 to 1913, we can only be impressed by the acuteness of his observations and the sagacity of his decisions. For they led him safely—indeed, triumphantly—through a period that was disastrous for most American architects and artists.

Wright's initial reactions were completely pragmatic. Escape from the eclecticism of the period was not merely an exercise in aesthetics, it was for him a matter of urgent, practical necessity. For the young architect discovered that, to build, he had to have materials. And in 1887 such materials as marble, brick, wood, bronze, velvet, and glass were all so tightly locked in corrupted design forms that their real, independent properties—color, texture, luster—were inaccessible. They had, indeed, become invisible. People could actually no longer see the marble for the column, the bronze for the vase, the wood for the jig-saw fretwork. Wright described the situation quite clearly: "Simple things . . . were nowhere at hand. A piece of wood without a moulding was an anomaly; a plain wooden slat instead of a turned baluster a joke; the omission of the merchantable 'grille' a crime; plain fabrics for hangings or floor covering were nowhere to be found in stock." Ornament had destroyed material, content was lost in bankrupt form.

The perception of this fact and the recognition of what must be done to escape its ugly consequences—these were

When in 1911 Wright began building Taliesin East (opposite), his own house near Spring Green, Wisconsin, the typical American living room was a clutter of bric-a-brac, mission furniture, and hideous wallpaper (right). He alone turned his back on tradition to reveal the inherent beauty of such materials as wood and stone.

what distinguished Wright from his contemporaries. Even Louis Sullivan, engaged in the same struggle, did not see the issue so clearly. In his attempt to replace bad ornament with good, Sullivan became obsessed with the problem—an obsession which led him ultimately into a dismal swamp of metaphysical speculation. Wright never made such an error. At first merely distrusting traditional ornament, he eventually came to despise it. The change, of course, does not occur overnight. In these early years we see his tentative efforts to adapt other men's styles to his own ends or to evolve equivalents of his own. We can easily trace this groping for a satisfactory system of expression and, in the process, we can see him experimenting with all the dominant architectural idioms of the day. Thus the first house he designed for himself (1889) is shingled Richardsonian; the Blossom house (1892), Colonial; the Harlan house (1892), Sullivanesque; the Bagley house (1894), Queen Anne; the Roloson row houses (1894) and the Moore house (1895), Tudor.

He tries each of these styles in turn; and the results, though derivative, are characterized by organizational firmness and clarity. But he does not repeat the experiment; these styles were clearly inadequate to his needs. We can also trace a parallel experimentation with the then-current styles in art, furniture, and interior décor. In the stair hall of his own house he uses a plaster frieze of classic figures. Over the playroom fireplace (1895) there is a flat mural of the Arabian Nights in a style reminiscent of Puvis de Chavannes. For the cornice of the Heller house (1897) he commissioned Richard Bock to do a terra-cotta frieze, a line of Beaux-Arts maidens embowered in Beardsley-Sullivan foliage. Throughout his interiors of this period we catch glimpses of Tiffany glass, tooled leather, stencil and appliqué, cattails and dried grasses—the echoes, in short, of William Morris.

But these borrowed and eclectic elements are always minor in his compositions, always handled with a restraint bordering on coolness. As the century closes, his architecture grows steadily more unified in expression, and such ornament and art as survive become less eclectic and more integral to the structure. His control over these art forms is increasingly apparent. Though he employed a number of artists and craftsmen in the decade between 1900 and 1910, his increasing editorship of their work is readily traced. In both subject matter and handling it moves toward simplification, toward abstraction. Stained glass, mosaic, frescoes, and wrought iron all show the influence of the Orient, especially of the Japanese print. Moreover, even big elements like the white wisteria mural in the Martin house (1904) or the lovely birch-and-fern panels in the Coonley living room (1907) are not independent statements on the part of free artists but are carefully subordinated to the requirements of the rooms. By the same token, freestanding sculpture and framed easel painting have now disappeared altogether. In the final large-scale project of the period—the Midway Gardens of 1913—there is a last great burst of sculpture, mural, and ornament;

CULVER SERVICE

but now it is art *designed* by the architect himself ("my own trusty T square and triangle" as he put it), and the sculptor is, in fact, merely the executor of the designs.

Fortunately for us, this developing attitude toward art and ornament is not only easily inferred from his successive buildings, it is also explicitly developed in his essays and speeches of the period. Indeed, these reveal the astonishing extent to which he rationalized the design process. They reveal a well-read intellectual (a role he was contemptuously to reject in later years) well aware of the artistic currents in his *ambiance*.

"The true value of a work of art," he told the Evanston University Guild in 1894, depends on its being "perfectly adjusted in relation to the whole, in absolute poise, leaving nothing but a feeling of quiet satisfaction." Evidently he found little that met this criterion, for two years later he told the same organization that he permitted "no prints or pictures [to] intrude upon attention" in his houses. They were not to imagine, however, that "pictorial art is banished." He would provide a cupboard to hold a portfolio of "print or etching, paint or water color." He would also provide somewhere a simple, dark-framed surface on which to display one "or perhaps two" of the best.

But the more he studied the art being offered to Chicagoans, the keener became his dissatisfaction. "A picture should be more than an imitation of a real object . . . more than a pretended hole in the wall, through which you see a story about something." Exasperation drives him still further in 1908: "Pictures deface walls oftener than they decorate them." Finally, two years later, he reaches the logical conclusion of this line of thinking. "The easel picture," he says flatly, "has no place on the walls. Great pictures should have their gallery. Oratorio is not performed in a drawing room."

This sort of generalized criticism of painting might, by itself, be dismissed as either parochial or misanthropic. But Wright did not stop with the general: he knew very well the art that was available to him, and his objections to it were concrete and specific. They dealt with both its form *and* its content. The forms "lacked repose"; they were strident, histrionic; they needed simplification, "conventionalizing." In short, they lacked that abstraction of reality which marked all great art. As for their subject matter: "The arts," he exclaims with wicked accuracy, "are today all cursed by literature; artists attempt to make literature even of music, usually of painting and sculpture and . . . of architecture also." The galleries and museums of Chicago were prison houses of gesture and anecdote, cast in forms of photographic artificiality. "Nature is never right for a picture," he tells one audience, "that is, not ready made." "If you see a picture in which perhaps a cow is looking out at you [so] 'real,' so 'lifelike,' " he tells another group sardonically, don't buy the picture—"buy the cow."

He had still deeper and more personal reservations. His revolt against the anecdotal in the work of such contemporaries as the preposterous Frederick William MacMonnies or the vacuous Kenyon Cox is quick and sure. But it is obvious that his distrust of the fine arts extended far beyond these pallid American expressions. In fact, as time goes on, his distrust

AARON SISKIND

Which of these houses is modern? The answer —strictly speaking—is neither one. Both are a half-century old. But the one at the far left, which more accurately reflected the taste of the time, now looks hopelessly old-fashioned with its turrets, cupolas, and haphazard ornamentation. On the other hand, Wright's famous Robie house on Chicago's South Side (near left) has a timeless quality that seems almost as "modern" today as it must have seemed in 1908.

extends to the whole tradition of Western art. Long before he saw Renaissance art at first hand, he was almost prudishly reacting against its "sensuality and extravagance." In 1908 he is urging "reticence in the matter of ornament. We crave ornament for the sake of ornament; cover up our faults of design with ornamental sensualities that were, a long time ago, sensuous ornamentation. . . . We will do well to distrust this unwholesome and unholy craving." The warning is more ethical than aesthetic.

Two years later, as a forty-year-old husband and father living near Florence with a woman not his wife, Frank Lloyd Wright stood face to face with the great artists of the Renaissance. He was stunned by their sensualism. "That splendid group of Florentine sculptors and painters and architects and sculptor-painters and painter-sculptors who were also architects" had erased the decent lines of distinction between the arts. He was forced to admit that "some of the sculpture is good painting; most of the painting is good sculpture; and in both lie the patterns of architecture." Nevertheless, he found it "as amazing as it is unfortunate." For despite its magnificent power and virtuosity, it was a "corrupt" art, confusing the "curious with the beautiful." Even worse, it was itself corrupting, leading to "the sensuality and extravagance of later periods." Out of the Renaissance had come the "debased" styles of baroque, rococo, Louis XIV; out of it ultimately had come the eclecticism that had submerged his own Chicago. Whatever its original intentions, however great its potentials, the Renaissance for Wright was a "soulless blight, a warning, a veritable damnation."

Strong words, these, with more than an echo of Cotton Mather. They reveal a very important aspect of Wright's personality. For despite a private life which, even then, was feeding many a lurid newspaper story, and despite a succession of designs that must rank among the most sensuously powerful in America—despite this, he remained at heart a Puritan. Here in Florence he was face to face with the fountainhead of that neoclassic current which had overwhelmed Louis Sullivan and even now threatened Wright. His rage is understandable. It must have seemed to him (and not without reason) that he alone, among the American architects, was fighting to establish an idiom of his own and was not, like them, a "parasite, feeding on past greatness."

If, then, neither the past nor the present of Western art was usable, what *was* an American architect in 1908 to do? A prophylactic measure would be to abjure ornament and decoration altogether: it was "dangerous . . . you are usually better off without it. . . . Look to the simple line, to the clean though living form, and quiet color." He himself was forced to follow this policy, he explained to a European audience in 1910, and that was why his own work lacked a "complete, highly developed" system of ornament. "Self-imposed limitations are in part responsible for this lack of intricate enrichment, and partly the imperfectly developed resources of our industrial system." And then this extremely significant statement: *"Tenderness has often to be sacrificed to integrity."* Thus, he says, he has forced himself to design buildings of a severely restrained nature "whose chief office is [to act as] a background or frame for the life within and about them." They are expressions of his conviction that "the ornamental forms of one's environment should be designed to wear well. [This] means that they must have absolute repose and make no especial claim upon attention; to be as far from realistic tendencies as a sense of reality can take them." His own houses, he says, must be understood in this light. They are "a serious attempt to formulate some industrial and aesthetic ideals that in a quiet, rational way will help to make a lovely thing of an American's home environment, produced without abuse by his own tools, and dedicated in spirit and letter to him."

Was this not sound advice for American artists and craftsmen in the first decade of the twentieth century? Wright is demanding no more of them than he rigorously demands of himself. His control of the birch-and-fern mural in the Coonley living room is no more severe than his control of the architecture of the room itself. Time is the acid test of such positions. What other living room of 1907 has worn as well as this? It must also be noted that he thought of his policy as temporary, a sort of cooling-off period, until artist and public alike would have been purged of corrupted taste: "ornament in the old sense is not for us yet." At the same time he understood quite well that the process of developing a whole new system of art forms, dedicated in letter and spirit to the modern American, could not be artificially speeded up. "All architecture worthy of the name is a growth, in accord with natural feeling and industrial means, to serve actual needs. It cannot be put on from without." It could only grow from within, "organically."

Writing of the early 1890's, Wright recalls in his autobiography that he could not endure the "realism" of American art as represented by such immensely popular works as the Rogers sculptural groups or such widely reproduced genre paintings as Hovenden's *Breaking Home Ties*. We can only praise his judgment here, but was his knowledge of *fin-de-siècle* American art really confined to such vernacular works as these? Had he never heard of Eakins, Ryder, Homer? Had no news of Whistler, Sargent, or Cassatt reached him on the shores of Lake Michigan? The same question must be asked concerning French painting: Was he the only person in Chicago who had never heard of Degas, Monet, Renoir? Was he alone ignorant of Cézanne, Van Gogh, Gauguin? Was this, in short, a personal provincialism or one he shared with his entire culture?

The facts seem to indicate that he was at least as well informed as the art experts who organized the great painting shows at the World's Columbian Exposition of 1893. One of these shows, "126 Foreign Masterpieces Owned by Americans," clearly indicated the limited knowledge and parochial taste of American collectors. To judge from it, these people were wholly ignorant of impressionist and postimpressionist painting; at least they showed no Frenchman later than Millet and Corot. As for the international show, it must have been an exercise in stupefying banality. Blashfield was there with a canvas called *Xmas Bells;* J. G. Brown showed his painting *The Card Trick;* other canvases by foreign artists were called variously *A Skating Party, Her First Born, The Blind at Church*. It is true that Homer, Eakins, Sargent, and Whistler were also there, obscurely hung and awarded minor prizes, and that Mary Cassatt had been commissioned to paint the north tympanum of the Women's Building. But the total impact of this art upon a young and perceptive sensibility could not have been less than traumatic: alone it would have been enough to explain Wright's lifelong distrust of Western painting.

Nor was the taste and knowledge of local experts any more sophisticated. In 1896 the Chicago Art Institute could not boast a single impressionist painting, though it did possess a Bouguereau and a Rosa Bonheur. By 1901 the Institute catalogue could list forty-odd Japanese prints and a single Whistler but nothing more advanced; and even as late as 1906 the Institute still did not possess a single School-of-Paris painting. It is true that some of the great Chicago collectors, Martin Ryerson among them, would shortly begin to buy impressionists; and the lordly Mrs. Potter Palmer, who chaired the Board of Lady Managers of the Exposition, already owned four Renoirs, several Monets, three Pissarros, and a Degas. But these arbiters of fashionable Chicago were the exception and, in any event, were far indeed above Wright's personal milieu. Despite a growing professional stature, his circle of friends and clients was still composed of middle-class professionals like himself—lawyers, doctors, newspaper editors. One of his few contacts with the world of great wealth and fashion came in 1907 when Harold McCormick commissioned him to design a house for a magnificent lake-shore site at Lake Forest. Had it been built, the project Wright evolved would have been one of the greatest country houses of all time; but it was apparently too advanced for Mrs. McCormick, who slipped off to New York one day and gave the commission to that impeccable eclectic, Charles Adams Platt. To exchange Wright for Platt was an eloquent index of upper-class Chicago taste, which was, as Sullivan had pointed out, increasingly and grossly subservient to an East it fancied to be more polished and secure.

Thus Wright appears no more limited in his knowledge of painting, and incomparably more advanced in his tastes, than those around him. Except for a handful of artists, no one in America was aware of the world-shaking events in France, and not until the great Armory Show of 1913 was the whole direction of American taste to be radically altered. What use Wright would have made of this art, had it been available to him then, is a matter of speculation. Certainly the artistic criteria of Gauguin, Van Gogh, and Matisse seem to us very similar to Wright's at the turn of the century, and it is pleasant to imagine an artistic union between them. Be that as it may, it is easy enough to understand why he rejected the painters and sculptors who *were* available to him. To whom, actually, could he have turned? To Kenyon Cox or Edwin

CONTINUED ON PAGE 127

CHICAGO ARCHITECTURAL PHOTOGRAPHING CO.

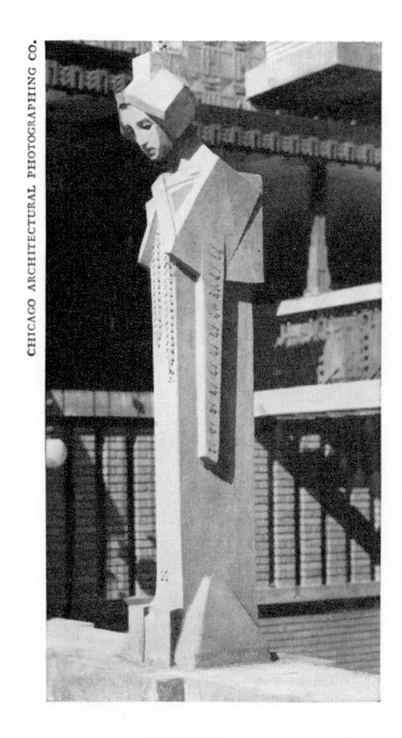

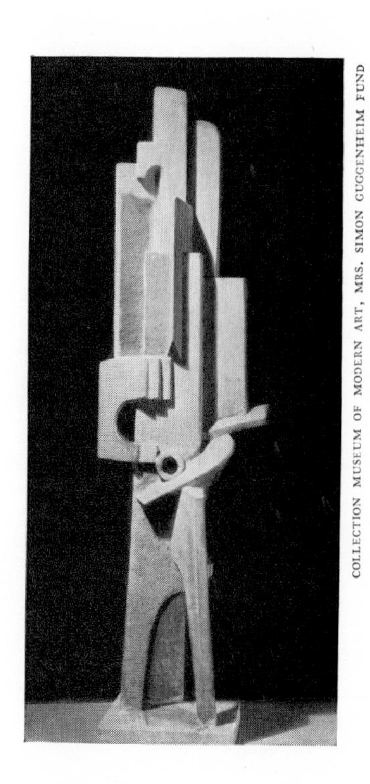

COLLECTION MUSEUM OF MODERN ART, MRS. SIMON GUGGENHEIM FUND

The banality of the art at the 1893 Columbian Exposition, like Karl Bitter's The Glorification of War *(center), led to Wright's lifelong distrust of painters and sculptors and to his reliance on his own talents. Thus he conceived, even if he did not himself execute, the caryatids (left) and the Kandinsky-like murals (below) for his Midway Gardens in 1913. One can only speculate on what he might have done had he been more aware of the artistic ferment in France and elsewhere, which in the same year produced Lipchitz's* Man with a Guitar *(right).*

JOHN LLOYD WRIGHT

COLLECTION OF MR. AND MRS. RICHARD F. SELIG

The French baroque mirror in Still Life with Angels *reflects the taste as well as the faces of John and Dora Koch. Other* objets d'art *in his painting are two angels from their Long Island summer place, an Oriental prayer rug, and an 18th-century bowl.*

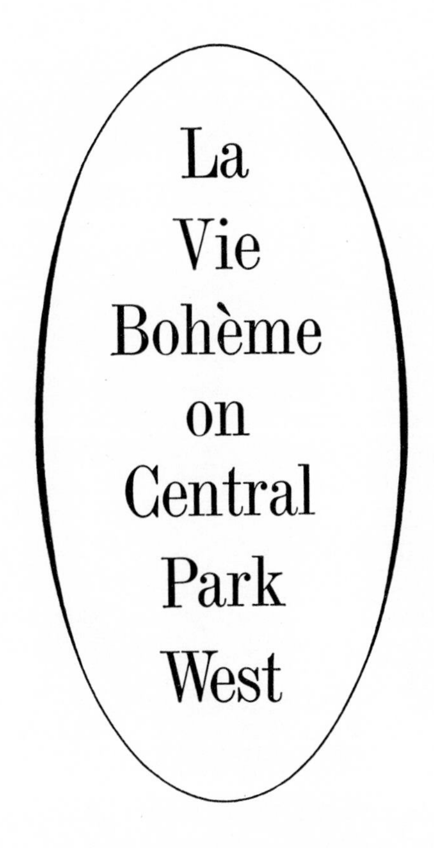

La Vie Bohème on Central Park West

Art mirrors life—and vice versa—in painter John Koch's polished household, a milieu that is about as far from the traditional garret as one can get

Some eighty New York City blocks separate the sumptuously appointed fourteen-room apartment of the painter John Koch on Central Park West from the stark lofts and bare pads downtown around Tenth Street that are favored by many of America's leading abstract expressionists. And a whole world of contrast separates his art and way of life from theirs.

A highly successful portraitist, Koch (pronounced Coke) is also a painter of genre pictures in a meticulous, realistic style whose atmosphere and use of light recall Vermeer's. The now little-practiced art of genre painting dwells on intimate, anecdotal details of everyday life; but the life of the Koch household, as the canvases reproduced on these pages portray it, is rather special. It is an opulent, many-sided, gregarious existence in a setting of elegance unusual among artists—in short, *la vie bohème de luxe.*

While the artist paints, his wife, Dora Zaslavsky, a pupil of Harold Bauer and Wilhelm Backhaus, gives advanced piano lessons at home and sometimes poses for him. Baroque mirrors, grand pianos, old masters, classical sculpture, Oriental *objets d'art,* and roomfuls of contemporary paintings—and people—surround them. Composers, writers, critics, pupils, patrons frequent the apartment in numbers: as many as ninety guests have been known to sit down for supper at the Kochs'. John Koch has not painted *that,* but in his group portrait (pages 106–107) he has characterized the hospitality of his expansive home.

Remarkably, the only formal art training the painter ever had was less than a year's study at fourteen in his home town of Ann Arbor, Michigan, under an Italian painter whom he disliked intensely and to whom, he says, "I was so sassy he threw me out of his studio." Unimpressed, Koch began

TEXT CONTINUED ON PAGE 111

By NELSON LANSDALE

Although the Kochs have given a great many parties, the one depicted here took place only on canvas. The guests posed for the painter separately and at different times. In the farther room are the painters Roger Baker and Maurice Grosser, in the doorway Dr. and Mrs. Leonard Smiley, and in the foreground the pianist Ania Dorfman and the critic Leo Lerman. The host has painted himself at the bar with Mrs. Edgar Feder. In the large group, from left to right, are composer Virgil Thomson; the late Noel Straus, music critic of the New York Times; *Mrs. Koch; in the chair, one of her pupils; painter Felicia Meyer Marsh (Mrs. Reginald Marsh); another of Mrs. Koch's pupils, with his back turned; painter Aaron Shikler; art dealer Roy Davis; butler Leroy Lowry; painter Raphael Soyer; and biographer Frances Winwar. The large baroque painting at right is an imaginary "old master" that Koch invented for his imaginary party. The small Vuillard to the left of it, though real enough, is from the collection of Mr. and Mrs. Ralph F. Colin (even though Koch has two Vuillards of his own).*

"COCKTAIL PARTY," COURTESY OF THE ARTIST

"STUDIO INTERIOR," COLLECTION OF MR. AND MRS. STANLEY GRUMBACHER

"MUSIC," KRAUSHAAR GALLERIES

"THE MOVERS," COLLECTION OF MR. AND MRS. EDWIN H. HERZOG

In his genre paintings John Koch records the debonair, art-centered life of his own household. Those on the opposite page show both of the Kochs at work—he in his studio (with two friends, painters Maurice Grosser and Roger Baker), she with one of her students, the pianist Abby Simon. Above, Mrs. Koch supervises the return of an old master from a loan exhibition, and below, tea is served in the drawing room after some chamber music.

"THREE MUSICIANS," KRAUSHAAR GALLERIES

COLLECTION OF MR. AND MRS. EDWIN H. HERZOG

During the summer of 1958 the Kochs occupied a flat in London's elegant Cadogan Square, where John painted himself reading the Times *while his wife goes over the morning mail.*

TEXT CONTINUED FROM PAGE 105

painting portraits of the citizenry of Ann Arbor, which his family had helped settle. Although Koch's parents were in easy circumstances, he began seeking his own livelihood in his teens "because I wanted to be on my own."

Today, at fifty-one, Koch is one of the top portrait painters in America, but his annual output of about twenty pictures is evenly divided between portraits and the genre pictures shown here. Normally there is a gap greater than the Grand Canyon between portrait painters and all other artists; but for Koch, the gap does not exist, thanks to his unusual approach to portraiture.

He arrived at this approach from Ann Arbor by way of Provincetown, where he studied with nobody "but learned a lot." By the time he was nineteen, he had made enough money from his portraits to plan a year in Europe. He stayed five, teaching himself to paint in the Louvre, not by the conventional copying but "by *looking at* pictures." Again, it was portraits that allowed him to live in comparative comfort, while on the side he flowed with current artistic tides, exhibiting in the Salon de Printemps and the Salon des Tuileries. Influenced successively by the Picasso of bleached bones on beaches, surrealism, symbolism, and Kandinsky's ideas of abstract art, he forced himself into the shape of the moderns of the period.

In 1933 he returned to America. In New York, he felt, he could be free of the shackles of the modern movement, with which he had never been really happy, and devote himself to realistic but romantic landscapes. The depression years of the thirties were no time for portraits by artists of small or no American reputation, but Koch's first one-man show anywhere, at the Valentine Gallery in 1935, which represented him as a "fine" (that is, non-portrait) artist, took care of that. It was very well received. The year 1935 also marked his marriage to Dora Zaslavsky, now one of New York's foremost teachers of music and a faculty member of the Manhattan School of Music.

Koch did not return to portraiture until the late 1930's, and his extraordinary success in the field since that time is due in part to the friendly personal relations he establishes with his sitters. Most portrait painters plop the subjects down in the artist's studio, with nothing around them expressive of themselves but the ball gown or the suit they happen to be wearing. A few rely on recordings to relax the subject.* Koch scorns such artificial stimuli and depends instead on conversation and his own easy charm to establish warm personal contact. He is likely to visit the subject's home, making dozens of quick sketches *in situ* for the backgrounds; the sitters themselves are almost invariably painted in his own studio, where the light is likely to be better and the paraphernalia of his craft are at hand. "They come at convenient morning hours, lunch with Dora and me, chat with her pupils, listen in on telephone conversations, and generally emerge feeling that they are part of the family." The artist adds, "I stay on the basis of very personal relations with them for years." And he paints them precisely as *he* pleases.

*See the article "Portraits in Our Time" by Eleanor C. Munro in HORIZON, January, 1959.

Koch would be the last to claim that he thought up this style of portraiture himself. It has a long pedigree going back to Flemish and Dutch masters like Frans Hals and Rembrandt, and in eighteenth-century England and France, "conversation pieces" in a comparable style were immensely popular. Koch has simply applied the principle to the twentieth century; if it is expensive for the client—his portraits cost from $4,000 to $15,000 and up, as against $1,800 to a top of $15,000 for the genre pictures like those presented here—it has enabled him to live in a style which at once brings to mind the princely town house in Antwerp of a seventeenth-century painter he worships—Peter Paul Rubens.

Koch is one of the few artists in America who is an important customer of the art dealers. His Central Park West apartment is hung with first-class paintings by El Greco, Tintoretto, the younger Canaletto, Ingres, Rubens, Boucher, Magnasco, Constable, Van Dyck; there are two Jan Steens, two Vuillards, four Guardis. Then, in addition to a roomful of the American Ashcan School (Sloan, Glackens, Prendergast, etc.), his collection of contemporaries includes major works by Walter Stuempfig, Leonid, Reginald Marsh, David Levine, Raphael Soyer, Louis Bouché, Isabel Bishop, and Edward Lanning. And among the younger painters represented on his walls are Roger Baker, Aaron Shikler, Gray Foy, Joe Lasker, John Heliker, and Noel Davis.

Between Koch's portrait subjects, his wife's piano students, and their general guests, the Central Park West apartment is a lively center of the creative arts. Its décor, as shown in these pictures, is mixed and lively, too, and belongs to no one particular period. The Kochs' Chippendale dining-room furnishings came from England; some of the best baroque furniture they acquired in Venice. And in his domestic paintings, Koch himself adds imaginatively to the mixture, as when he includes a pair of sculptured angels (page 104) that hang not in his New York apartment but in his summer house in Setauket, Long Island, or when he represents as hanging on his wall, paintings that happen to belong to friends of his and that are hanging on *their* wall, or when, finally, in depicting his own living room he simply invents an imaginary old master (pages 106–107)—as if he didn't have enough of his own. All this, in turn, reflects the general exuberance of John Koch's life and art.

If you ask him why he paints as he does in the face of the present-day avalanche of abstract expressionism, his answer is simple: "It's the most natural and expressive way for me; realism is my natural vehicle, but that doesn't mean I think everybody else should do it." His realism is that of his own particular atmosphere and the people and enthusiasms that compose it.

Nelson Lansdale, a free-lance writer, contributed "Mrs. Gardner's Palace of Paintings" to the July, 1959, HORIZON.

BILL CHARMATZ

THEATER

By ROBERT HATCH

LAUGHTER AT YOUR OWN RISK

Sleep is lovely, death is better still, not to have been born is of course the miracle.

I quote these lines from Heine, as recently translated by Robert Lowell, because I'm tired of people pinching their mouths at Samuel Beckett for celebrating the nausea of existence. Most men feel it, certainly all poets do—Heine's lines are a paraphrase of Sophocles—and it has nothing to do with despair, which is the related charge leveled against Beckett. He states his case—the most recent of many similar statements—in a one-character, one-act play, *Krapp's Last Tape,* which opened last January at the Provincetown Playhouse in New York's Greenwich Village. As I expect to make clear shortly, the hero of *Krapp's Last Tape* has been trapped in a cage for thirty years, but I doubt that the least sensitive member of the audience would care to put his arm through those bars. Krapp has the stare of a badger; despair has not tamed it.

It is curious about Beckett that, though he deals in the most dire experience, his fables do not depress. There is a salty virility to his people, an assumption of equality with juggernaut, that gives off the exciting smell of human pride. "Use your head," says Hamm in Beckett's play *Endgame,* "use your head, can't you, you're on earth, there's no cure for that!" No more is there, but it does not occur to a Beckett character to take that grim fact lying down.

Figuratively speaking, that is. His heroes are not infrequently lying down

Krapp's delight as he savors the word "Spooool!" is captured in Philippe Halsman's photo of the actor Donald Davis.

when we first meet them. Prone or supine—Beckett's people give a good deal of thought to the relative advantages of the two positions. Supine, one enjoys a breadth of vision, but prone, one can get over the ground more readily, gripping with the knees and digging forward with the fingernails. Proceeding that way, you may advance a good twenty yards in a day, and who's to say that a man should reasonably aspire to more. The hub of Beckett's insight—the recurring vision of the recent novels: *Molloy, Malone Dies, The Unnamable*—is that experience is subjective, inviolable, and immeasurable. Molloy, finding himself on the beach, gathers a little trove of sixteen stones, admirable for sucking, and works out a procedure for enjoying them in orderly rotation. Is this an achievement of less stature than Newton's formulation of the laws of motion? Well, that would depend on whether you put your question to Newton or to Molloy. Or do you say that society will judge such matters? I refrain from telling you what Molloy would say if you came at him with a word like "society."

Or consider Malone, also representing the human race. He is almost dead when we first encounter him, and at the end, there is just the difference that he is quite dead. He lies on a bed, he knows not where; brought to this pass, he knows not how; fed by anonymous hands that come no more. He has possessions—one yellow shoe, a hat with the brim gone, a photograph of a donkey with downcast eyes, a needle embedded in two corks, a scrap of newspaper, a stone—and these he can reach and stir with a long stick, for he enjoys the use of his arms. In bed with him are two pencils, one of which he can no longer find, and a notebook. That is important, for in the time left to him Malone will tell stories—write them, rather, because the "others do not endure, but vanish, into thin air." Then he will make an inventory of his possessions, and then he will die. I cannot possibly say whether we are with him for twenty minutes, or two months, or ten years. What I can be sure of is that the acquaintance is amusing and enriching. That virtual corpse, abandoned in a bed on casters, is an adventurer and commander to shadow Alexander. I am not trafficking in paradoxes; Malone is man stripped to artist. We are the only animal that sings its own saga, and which is more important, the singing or the doing? It is immaterial in Malone's case, for he *does* in order to sing. He grasps life because it gives him a story to tell, and when it is done, he is done. Malone, infinitely vulnerable and infinitely tough: "This club is mine. . . . It is stained with blood, but insufficiently, insufficiently. I have defended myself, ill, but I have defended myself."

With Krapp, though, the adventure is different. The others—Malloy, Malone, Hamm, etc.—as good as dead to begin with, live off the transfusions of their art. Krapp, on the contrary, suffers art to cut him down in his prime and then lives on to see himself as a mirror of snapshots receding through the years. If science has its martyrs, so does art—men withered by the invisible, burning rays. Krapp, I believe, is one of these.

Krapp's Last Tape is the outrageous title of an outrageous play. Imagine! A feeble, nearly blind and deaf, solitary and half-drunk old man, crouching in a squalid room, subsisting on bananas and playing to himself (commenting the while) old tape recordings of his own voice—recordings, moreover, that consist in no small part of comments on still earlier tapes. Is this theater? Well, yes, it is; outrageous, of course, but very much theater. Being outrageous in the theater is nothing new for Beckett. There was that matter of Godot who never showed up, and of the animated *Endgame*, three of whose four characters were immobilized, and two of those in ash cans. Another play, among Beckett's many, that I would dearly love to see, is *Act Without Words I*. It takes place in a featureless desert and involves the pantomime of a man beset by objects—a tree, a pair of scissors, a carafe of water, a knotted rope, etc., all lowered from the flies—and by a commanding whistle that emanates from various points off stage. It reads as though it would play like man's fate, caught beneath a burning glass.

These capers of Beckett's are a function of his virtuosity. He plays in the theater as a hawk plays in the air currents—with the exuberance of being at home. Beckett carries a stage within his head. When he writes a scene, he knows how it will materialize, how long it will take, where its center of gravity will lie, what impact it will make. This is something outside, in addition to, the dialogue—it is the kinetic sense of the theater. O'Neill, I would guess, was like that. When Donald Davis, who created the role of Krapp in New York, and Alan Schneider, who directed him in it (and directed also, in earlier seasons, *Waiting for Godot* and *Endgame*), began to move the old man around the stage, they found that Beckett already had the whole piece moving in the script. Every pause, every repetition, every agonized progress from A to B had been timed with that enigmatic metronome which sets a play's pace. This sort of thing: *. . . fumbles in his pockets, encounters the banana, takes it out, peers at it, puts it back, fumbles, brings out the envelope, fumbles, puts back envelope, looks at his watch, gets up and goes backstage into darkness. Ten seconds. Sound of bottle against glass, then brief siphon. Ten seconds. Bottle against glass alone. Ten seconds. He comes back a little unsteadily. . . .**

When Schneider and Davis stuck to the letter of such instructions, the play marched. When they experimented with sequence, or invented or subtracted, the action stalled. They added an overhead light and, in correspondence with Beckett, worked out some business to italicize a phrase they feared the American audiences would ride over. Otherwise they worked as did Toscanini with a score—they materialized what was given.

Acting in a one-part play is an odd experience. Davis, who talks of *Krapp's Last Tape* with loving possessiveness—it has been, after all, *his* play, in a way not often given to an actor—says that the problem is to keep the acting alive, performance after performance. In the theater, he says, you expect to feel minute differences, from evening to evening, in the thrust and parry of your colleagues, and adjusting to these keeps the blood running in your own performance. With *Krapp's Last Tape* there is only the recording machine for foil, and it makes the problem the more difficult, for it never varies by a hair or a decibel. (Most spectators, by the way, assume that the machine on stage is a dummy and that the sound is controlled by a hand off stage. Beckett, who had never seen a tape recorder, thought it could be worked that way, but Davis and Schneider found that, what with the repeats and jumps called for in the script, the hazards of synchronization were too great. During the long rehearsals, Davis acquired Krapp's own cranky mastery of the gadget, slapping it around as he would a wife who had lost her charm and putting it scornfully through its paces.)

The resilient give-and-take that Davis needed in the months of his performance (he left the play late in the spring to join the American Shakespeare Festival at Stratford, Connecticut) was supplied in large part by Schneider, who, whatever his other projects, made a practice of dropping in on the show every few days. Once, when Schneider was out of town for a time, Davis felt his performance slipping and could not put his finger on the trouble. Schneider spotted it his first evening back in town. Davis is a vigorous man of thirty-two; Krapp, a phenomenon of decrepitude ("The sour curd and the iron stool"), is sixty-nine. The strain of maintaining this gap of years is considerable, and Davis, with no one to react against, had been lopping the years off.

There is no curtain at *Krapp's Last Tape*. When you take your seat, a dark fusty room confronts you. There is a table at stage center, with a recorder and some cardboard boxes on it, a light overhead, a shabby chair alongside. That is all you can see, and you can imagine what you care to imagine beyond vision. After a time the lights go down. When they come up again, Krapp sits in the chair (in a coma?), the recorder cover in his lap. It is his birthday, the one day each year when he records a new tape. He sits there a moment, staring blindly, and then begins one of those great vaudeville pantomimes that are Beckett's hallmark: the fumble through the pockets, the watch held painfully to the eye, the aimless shifting of papers, the bunch of keys to the eye, the right key in the fingers, the shuffle around the table (good God, the painful shuffle!) to the first drawer. Unlock the drawer, open it, peer in, pull out a tape, hold it up to the light, put it back, close the drawer, lock it; keys to the eye again, select another, open the second drawer, peer in, feel around with the paw, out comes a banana (laughter—you always laugh at your own risk at a Beckett play), hold up the banana (Beckett says in a letter to Schneider that Krapp displays objects with the overwinning candor of a stage magician showing his innocent props), close drawer, lock it, keys back in the pocket, straighten up and face audience, stroke the banana, peel it, drop skin to floor, stick banana into mouth and stare vacantly into space (you may be wishing now that you could have your laugh back), suddenly chomp down on it and gobble with soft eagerness (no teeth), pacing the while. Stumble on the banana peel (of course), kick it into the pit, finish the fruit, hobble back to the chair, full stop. Then a sigh, then out with the keys and up to the eye, and we're off again. Not quite the same, though, for this time he re-

*The quotations in this article are from *Krapp's Last Tape and Other Dramatic Pieces* published by Grove Press, New York, 1960.

sists the banana even after it is in his mouth (a tape of thirty years ago, which Krapp eventually will play, says, "Have just eaten I regret to say three bananas and only with difficulty refrained from a fourth. Fatal things for a man with my condition. . . . Cut 'em out!"). He stows the banana in a vest pocket. (This became an increasing trial to Davis last spring, and on some evenings he omitted the rediscovery of the banana.) Krapp shuffles off with lunatic briskness into the darkness and a cork pops—the first of several such pops from the dark. He emerges with an old ledger, puts it on the table, wipes his mouth with his hand, his hand on his coat, and rubs the hands briskly together. Life, it appears, is about to begin.

What life? Why, the only life that matters to this diseased, dirty, drunken old hermit—the recording of Krapp's story. But Krapp has no story. What he has is the iteration of a spot on a tape where experience got stuck thirty years ago. Krapp, as I have said, is a martyr to art, one who was burned. It is dangerous work—we've known that from as long ago as the caves—but we choose to overlook the hazards, for we need the product.

Had Krapp been an artist? Quite probably—at least he was a man overwhelmed by language: the sound of words, their power to make experience real, their power, in the end, to supplant experience. In fact, Krapp was too vulnerable to words; he should never have taken up the trade.

There are all sorts of signs. Looking up the tape he wants in the ledger, Krapp reads out (they are his first words): "Ah! Box . . . thrree . . . spool . . . five." Abruptly his head goes up, he listens, and then, "Spool! Spooool!" The sound spirals out and up like a lovely curl of light—the sensuality of words. After much more business with boxes, keys, and drawers, he locates the tape and flings it on the recorder like a practiced but drunken engineer. When it has been running a while, with pauses for Krapp to savor the old presence of himself, this passage occurs:

"*. . . there is of course the house on the canal where mother lay a-dying, in the late autumn, after her long viduity . . .*"
Krapp starts up, switches off, reels back again: "*. . . after her long viduity.*" He switches off, stares, tries the word on his lips, gets up (no joke for him), stumbles off and comes back with a dictionary—an unabridged—lays it on the table, and fumbles through the pages: "*State—or condition of being—or remaining—a widow—or widower.* (Looks up. Puzzled.) *Being—or remaining? . . . Also of an animal, especially a bird . . . the vidua or weaver-bird . . . Black plumage of male . . .* (He looks up. With relish.) *The vidua-bird!*"
The audience laughs over "spooool" and "viduity" as over the banana. Quite right; it is very funny business—but there is also a chill to it.

Krapp speaks well—that is the link between the youth, the man, and the old wreck. Words are his tools: a nursemaid (she had threatened to call the police when he had spoken to her) has eyes "like crysolite"; a ball he is throwing for a dog is a "small, old, black, hard, solid rubber ball"; the shade on his mother's death-room window is "one of those dirty brown roller affairs." Words, it seems, are taking over; "crysolite" is more important than the policeman, the characteristics of the shade weigh more than the death.

See what happens. The tape of thirty years ago spins on:
"*. . . at the end of the jetty, in the howling wind, never to be forgotten, when suddenly I saw the whole thing. The vision, at last. This I fancy is what I have chiefly to record this evening, against the day when my work will be done and perhaps no place left in my memory, warm or cold, for the miracle that . . .* (hesitates) *. . . for the fire that set it alight. What I suddenly saw then was this, that the belief I had been going on all my life, namely—*"

But Krapp will not listen; angrily he switches off and reels ahead, picking up:
"*. . . clear to me at last that the dark I have always struggled to keep under is in reality my most—*"
Krapp curses and reels on:
"*. . . unshatterable association until my dissolution of storm and night with the light of the understanding and the fire—*"
This is awful; he can't get away from it. Cursing and reeling ahead, he comes at last on a passage he will play again and again. It deals with yet another occasion. I won't quote much of it; there is the danger, when you start quoting Beckett, of going on to the end. He makes a kind of poetry. But the Krapp of those days was in a punt with a girl:
"*. . . I noticed a scratch on her thigh and asked her how she came by it. Picking gooseberries, she said. I said again I thought it was hopeless and no good going on, and she agreed, without opening her eyes.* (Pause.) *I asked her to look at me and after a few moments—* (pause)*—after a few moments she did, but the eyes just slits, because of the glare. I bent over her to get them in the shadow and they opened.* (Pause. Low.) *Let me in.* (Pause.) *We drifted in among the flags and stuck. The way they went down, sighing, before the stem! . . .*"

And so on. It is beautifully stated, and it is the end of Krapp, aged thirty-nine. What he had discovered that night on the jetty he can no longer bear to remember. Lies, probably the death of life. Whatever it was, it led him soon thereafter to that suicide in the punt. Men live their lives; artists must both live and celebrate; those who are destroyed by art celebrate instead of living. For Krapp reality became not the punt and the girl and the sun and the flags—but the tape that records those things. Now, thirty years later, when he takes up the microphone to record:
"*Nothing to say, not a squeak. What's a year now? . . . Revelled in the word spool.* (With relish.) *Spooool! Happiest moment of the past half million.*"
Then he puts on the old tape again, and the last we see of him he is lying with his head on the machine as the voice memorializes that afternoon and ends:
"*Perhaps my best years are gone. When there was a chance of happiness. But I wouldn't want them back. Not with the fire in me now. No, I wouldn't want them back.*"

Krapp's Last Tape is a sad play for anyone; for artists it could be an object of terror. What it means to Beckett, I shall not presume to say, but I could guess that it represents a nightmare escaped. People are always comparing Beckett with Joyce: they are both Irish, and Beckett is said to have served as Joyce's secretary. In fact, his debt to Joyce is no greater than that of half the writers in his generation, and as for working for him, Beckett says he used sometimes to write letters for him or run literary errands—as did a good many in the English and American colony in Paris of those days. There are, for example, only two references to Beckett in Joyce's letters. One related that Beckett had devised an acrostic on Joyce's name; Beckett says now that he cannot even remember how it went.

What is forgotten is that Beckett's second book was a study of Proust, written in 1931, before any of his novels or plays. After that he wrote for twenty years with almost no recognition. Krapp, shifting around the table, dislodges a little pile of books. He picks one up: *"Seventeen copies sold, of which eleven at trade price to free circulating libraries beyond the seas. Getting known."* This remembrance of things past also brings a laugh.

When you realize that Beckett was forty-six before *Godot* threw him a bridge to the world, you may guess why the unappetizing Krapp, with his bananas and his "spooools," his "viduity," his "crysolite," his visions on the jetty and renunciations in the punt, crawls with such terrifying authority through his litter of impoverishment: *"Sometimes wondered in the night if a last effort mightn't—*(Pause.) *Ah finish your booze now and get to your bed. Go on with this drivel in the morning. Or leave it at that. Leave it at that."*

An artist may go on for quite a time, seeing himself as Molloy or Malone or whichever of those clowns and desperate pilgrims crying out their stories in a lunar landscape. But when he sees himself as Krapp in his den, cursing and drinking and searching out the right word, fighting terror—"Last fancies. (*Vehemently.*) Keep 'em under!"—and recording new reflections of old reports of sterile years; when that is the way he sees himself, he is going down for the third time. No wonder the play fascinates—we are always asking one another what it must feel like to die.

MOVIES

By JEAN STAFFORD

THREE ORPHANS AND THEIR PATRON SAINT

A press release from the Disney studio concludes, with a humid eye and a choked voice, that *Pollyanna* is a "picture that will be shown all over the world for years to come, carrying with it an electrifying philosophy and a heart-warming beauty." The picture is, indeed, easy on the eye: it is almost impossible not to be pleased with a setting in a small New England town in 1912 in summer when big trees dapple white houses and wide lawns; minutes away from Main Street (where prosperous matrons emerge from electric cars, wearing botanical hats and buttoned kid gloves and carrying parasols) there are limpid streams and mossy dingles and amber waves of grain, all flourishing under the true-blue spacious skies of America the beautiful.

Thanks to David Swift, the director who also wrote the script, and to Hayley Mills, who plays the title role of orphan Pollyanna, the "electrifying philosophy" —an early precursor of positive thinking evolved by probably the most poisonous child in all of fiction—does not electrocute the audience; it merely, on occasion, numbs.

I had been much impressed by Miss Mills, a fourteen-year-old Londoner, in her performance as a rag-tag-and-bobtail Cardiff waif who befriends a murderer in *Tiger Bay*. And now her achievement in this great gelatinous pudding of schmalz convinces me that she is a genius, and if she is not debilitated or saccharified by Hollywood, we will be watching a great actress for a long time. Even in her conversion of Adolphe Menjou from a beastly old curmudgeon to a lovable old curmudgeon, she does not nauseate; and her intelligence and style prevail when she is explaining the origin of her "glad game" to querulous, selfish, hypochondriacal Agnes Moorehead. As the child of a poor but honest clergyman in the West Indies (now in heaven), she longed for a doll, and her loving, indigent father wrote to a Ladies Aid asking if they could spare a used, beat-up one for his Pollyanna. Well, sir, there was a mix-up and instead of a doll, our heroine got a pair of crutches. But though she was keenly disappointed, she was at the same time glad because she wasn't crippled and didn't need the orthopedic supplies. I can think of almost no other scene in literature so challenging, and Hayley Mills accepts the challenge with such sterling talent that she remains real and likable. (One blushes to think of this scene in the original version which starred Mary Pickford, America's sweetheart. Mary must have been about twenty-five then, and a real doll.) I saw *Pollyanna* at a screening for New York high-school editors, and a tough, cynical lot they appeared to be as I observed them before the lights went off.

I expected hisses and rude laughter; there were none, but I am sure there would have been if this remarkable child had not outwitted Eleanor H. Porter, the creator of the odious Goody Two-shoes.

Pollyanna's chum is an orphan boy in eleemosynary knickerbockers and he is played by Kevin Corcoran, who is eleven. He is overshadowed by the star in this picture, but I saw him some months ago in *Toby Tyler,* another Disney production, and he convinced me, although I had the feeling that he may not be an actor when he ceases to be a child, whereas Hayley Mills, if she is allowed to grow naturally, will be an actress all her life. *Toby Tyler* is another period piece, circa 1890, chockablock with tried and tested clichés most of which work quite as well as ever. Toby Tyler, an orphan (Kevin Corcoran is a repeating or double-barreled orphan and Disney is the patron saint of orphans) who lives with a crosspatch uncle and a thin-lipped aunt, runs away from home and joins a circus. He rises from peanut vendor to star trick horseback rider in nothing flat, realizing the dream of all American children in the days when circuses were in tents and smelled like circuses. Under the Strong Man's rough exterior there beats a heart of solid gold; the clown is a saint; the concessionaire, Toby's first employer, is a crook in a straw hat and arm bands, and he gets his comeuppance in the end for his double-dealing despite his clever spiel; the harsh foster parents see Toby's performance, smile proudly, and agree that they have misjudged him.

Toby and a chimpanzee, after an initial altercation over a banana which the latter steals, become the best of friends, and there is one scene involving the pair that I found altogether masterful, wonderfully comic in itself besides being a spoof of westerns. It is the Fourth of July, and as the circus parade proceeds down the main street of a small town, some prankster throws a string of small firecrackers (known as "ladycrackers" in my day) into the wagon in which the Strong Man, Toby, and Mr. Stubbs, the chimp—so called because he reminds Toby of someone back home—are riding. Mr. Stubbs panics and thereby panics the horses; the wagon overturns and Toby is hurled to the ground. He sees stars only for a moment, for he realizes that Mr. Stubbs has disappeared. Mr. Stubbs, meanwhile, has taken over the sheriff's office and there he sits in a swivel chair, terrorizing the citizenry by shooting a six-gun through the door and windows and taking pot shots at two prisoners in their cells. With relief, the embattled and evicted sheriff ducks the last bullet, but Mr. Stubbs swivels the chair around and picks another gun out of a pigeonhole in a roll-top desk. It is Toby Tyler, of course, who disarms him and restores law and order to the town. In the book *Toby Tyler,* Mr. Stubbs is fatally shot by a hunter, but Disney, with his infallible way of winning friends and influencing people, suffers him only to receive a flesh wound which will be set right in a jiffy by the clown, who seems to hold a degree from the New York State Veterinary College of Cornell University.

Despite their blatant sentimentality and their absolute want of subtlety, both these gorgeously colored, upholstered movies are fun, and I enjoyed them as I enjoyed movies when I was a child. One should really eat popcorn at them in order to bring out the full flavor of the corn on the screen. When movier movies are made, Disney will make them. Most Hollywood movies these days aren't movie enough.

BOOKS

By GILBERT HIGHET

LIFE BEHIND THE IVY

It is a pleasantly familiar setting: the walls of mellow brick or venerable gray stone; the green lawns, crisscrossed, as the bell sounds the hour, by cheerful youngsters laden with books and grave oldsters laden with learning; the lights glowing steadily at night in library and laboratory; the clack of typewriters and the hum of IBM machines in the central administration building; the discreetly sumptuous mansion where the loneliest man in the university entertains an endless stream of strangers; and, at the end of each year, the little miracle which, for a day, transforms the fresh-faced young into sober black-clad graduands, and their teachers, usually haggard and harassed, into a pageant as hieratic and radiant as a stained-glass window. The college, or the university, was once a world apart: a small, precious, spiritual retreat which showed no hospitality to the profane, scarcely acknowledging their existence; a self-perpetuating community with its own property, its own laws, and its own language. But now, more and more in every generation and most of all in ours, it has been changing into an integral part of the nation. Here in the United States, and in some other countries, young men go to college whose great-grandfathers scarcely managed to attend elementary school; and girls go to college whose great-grandmothers would have been forbidden to think of such a thing. University teachers, driven by poverty, ambition, or the teaching impulse, no longer keep themselves aloof. They work for the government, sometimes in the government; they travel abroad on official missions; they arbitrate public issues; they write books which people can actually read.

Books are written about them, too. In these last few years there have been a surprising number of novels about college and university life, and more are appearing every year, both in the United States and in Britain. Some of these stories are brilliantly accurate. Others are brilliantly distorted. For nearly everyone who has been to college, and surely for everyone who lives and works in a university, they are all captivating.

The worst thing that can happen in a university is the deliberate perversion of its ideals. Therefore the most serious academic theme for a novelist is intellectual corruption. This is the subject of C. P. Snow's latest tale, *The Affair*. Its setting is a small, rich, honorable college of Cambridge University. A young Fellow of the college has been charged with faking a distinguished scientific discovery by forging the photographic evidence, and has, after a trial, been expelled. Was he guilty, we are asked as the novel opens, or not guilty? All universities try to hush up degrading internal scandals, and the British are rather better at hush-work than other nations; so the affair was heard *in camera,* kept out of the papers, and forgotten. The scientist himself, a surly young boor at best, sits silent among the ruins of his shattered career. But his dogged and voluble wife forces a few of his colleagues to reopen the case. Reexamined, the Affair seems far more difficult than the original verdict made it appear. True, the victim cannot speak for himself, or will not: perhaps as a scientist he is naturally inarticulate, perhaps as a Communist fellow traveler he scorns such bourgeois conventions as frankness and civility. Perhaps, again, he was really innocent, and is now contemptuously silent because he despises everyone connected with the injustice that broke his life. Perhaps the evidence against him was inadequately examined; possibly he was incapable of defending himself; conceivably he was—

The word "framed" would scarcely be used in official discussions by the Fellows of a Cambridge college; but the concept is known and the stratagem is not inconceivable. Was the man framed? If so, who is to judge the appeal now lodged against his expulsion? The senior Fellows, who were deceived during his first trial? The man, or men, who contrived the evidence against him? With these problems, C. P. Snow confronts his readers and subtly leads them into the labyrinth of human motives. Ambition, prudence, pride, probity, hatred—they interweave like the forces of a difficult chess problem; and, when the solution emerges, we see that a few small acts of negligence, misplaced loyalty, and subtle deceit have changed the lives of several score of men and women and have endangered the honor of a noble institution.

In a crisis as grave as that of *The Affair* (or of its slightly cruder but sometimes richer predecessor, Eleazar Lipsky's *The Scientists*), university life, normally so bland of surface, becomes a succession of problems and combats. But without such a crisis, what is it? Many novelists think it is funny.

Irreverent writers have therefore produced some delicious caricatures of those desiccated, bespectacled nymphs and frustrated, evasive satyrs who inhabit "the groves of Academe." The phrase comes from Horace; it reminds the informed reader that the first of all Western colleges was founded by Plato in a grove sacred to the almost unknown hero Akademos, and that Mary McCarthy chose it as the title of a brilliant academic satire published in 1952. Her scene is a terribly progressive girls' college—or should we say a girls' terribly progressive college? Her perception of the foibles of its inhabitants and visitors is devastatingly funny and couched, as usual, in brightly faceted, sharply edged prose; and the gimmick, or twist, in her plot is sophisticated in the extreme. The president of the college feels he ought to fire an exceptionally indolent, objectionable, and inefficient teacher; but he dare not, because the teacher is a Communist: so he himself resigns. This—although written earlier—looks like a neatly satiric parody of the problem analyzed in C. P. Snow's *The Affair*. Just as Cambridge is the antithesis of Jocelyn College, Jocelyn, Pennsylvania, so in Cambridge it is uncomfortable and even dangerous to be a fellow traveler, while in Jocelyn it almost ensures respect and tenure.

Miss McCarthy's satire was not only witty in itself, but the cause of wit in others. It evoked another satire, written with equal grace and originality, depending very little on anything so crude as a story line but containing what might be interpreted as a crushing satiric portrait of someone very like Miss McCarthy herself. This novel was Randall Jarrell's *Pictures from an Institution,*

A PICTURE OF

If Benton [College] had had an administration building with pillars it could have carved over the pillars: *Ye shall know the truth, and the truth shall make you feel guilty.* Just as ordinary animal awareness has been replaced in man by consciousness, so consciousness had been replaced, in most of the teachers of Benton, by social consciousness. They were successful in teaching most of their students to say in contrition, about anything whatsoever: *It was I, Lord, it was I;* but they were not so successful in teaching them to consider this consciousness of guilt a *summum bonum,* one's final claim upon existence. Many a Benton girl went back to her nice home, married her rich husband, and carried a fox in her bosom for the rest of her life—and short of becoming a social worker, founding a Neo-Socialist party, and then killing herself and leaving her insurance to the United Nations, I do not know how she could have got rid of it.

The people of Benton had not all been provincial to begin with, but they had made provincials of themselves, and first published in 1954. It is a lovely book, with many epigrams, a few very funny students, and a truly wonderful Viennese musician called Rosenbaum; but one wonders whether all the characters are identifiable with real academic personages, and if so, with whom.

At this point, when academic fiction becomes as obscure as this, it is really turning its back on the world. It closes the campus gates firmly behind itself, draws the curtains, and talks in a special language about its own special people. Almost the extreme of satiric privacy is reached in *The Party at Cranton* by John W. Aldridge, published in the spring of 1960. Gossip suggests that this is meant to be, at least in part, a satire on Kenyon College, a highly reputed intellectual oasis in the Middle West; that the leading figure, a transplanted Southerner called Arthur Keith Buchanan, bears a close resemblance to a critic especially prominent in little-review circles; and that the other figures (among whom we see the gleaming smile of a lady satirist) are recognizable, though acridly unsympathetic, portraits of the members of a single institution. The book is amusing to read, although rather painful, for it is a carefully constructed killing-trap, full of sharp and poisonous epigrams. Yet since most of its readers (unless its sale is unexpectedly small) have never been to Kenyon, or met the intellectuals who populate it, or even read their works, they will see *The Party at Cranton* less as a satire than as a set of crazy and unconvincing charades.

Had it been less full of hate and scorn, more appreciative of the absurd, it might have been a good institutional comedy, aimed not at destroying pretentious individuals but at enjoying ridiculous types. Such comedies are Vladimir Nabokov's *Pnin* (which surely carries a wry smile in its very name), Kingsley Amis's *Lucky Jim* (which is a perfect manual of how to achieve failure as a college instructor), and Malcolm Bradbury's new comedy, *Eating People Is Wrong.* (This contains a particularly endearing picture of an African potentate who is studying at a British university in order to return home and become an anti-British terrorist. When the Vice-chancellor discovers him locked into one of the university lavatories and asks, "Who is to blame for this?" he replies, "Society.")

Reliability and maturing wisdom, rather than driving self-centered energy, are the qualities of most university teachers. There are many who want only tranquillity and security, without responsibility; yet some are driven by ambition, whether it be the lust for power over men and institutions or the simpler yearning for titles, privileges, and praise. The effects of ambition in an academic community are beautifully worked out, on very different canvases, by Carlos Baker of Princeton in *Friend in Power* and by C. P. Snow of Cambridge in his earlier academic novel, *The Masters.* In both books, a group of men in middle life are competing with one another to become the head of a great institution. But the difference between them is typical of the difference between Britain and America. In the American novel everything is rather too large and amorphous; in the British novel everything is too small and constricted. The search for a new president of the university, in Carlos Baker's story, ranges far and wide over scores of possibilities, and at last we are astonished, though pleased, to see the choice fall on a professor who has been one of the searchers. In *The Masters* there are only four possible candidates, only fifteen electors; the negotiations are informal, apparently almost offhand; when the final choice is made, the accidents of personality have combined to influence it, and yet something like an abstract principle has decided the issue.

The odd thing is that none of these books tells us much about the mass population of colleges and universities—the students: how they are taught, how disciplined, and how they feel about both their teachers and the adventure of learning. There are very few novels which tell us about the life of the student. Yale is a rather conservative institution and so, in its own way, is Oxford, but both *Zuleika Dobson* and *Stover at Yale* are out of date: charming, no doubt, but charming as antiques. Here there is a fine field open for a novelist who is young enough to remember, old enough to understand, and self-disciplined enough to refrain from the usual excesses of egoism. Also we need several novels on the career and personality of a university teacher. At present I know of no single book—unless perhaps the forgotten *Mad Professor* of Hermann Sudermann—which portrays such a teacher with all his frustrations and exultations. And we need a novel on the life of the president of a great university—someone like Nicholas Murray Butler or Charles William Eliot. Such men were stronger and stranger than most academic characters invented by novelists; and the only things we miss in their autobiographies and official life histories are the qualities forbidden to scholars and university administrators: complete frankness and the graces of a sensitive, individual style.

AN INSTITUTION

called their province, now, the world. And it was a world in which almost nothing happened, a kind of steady state. Benton was a progressive college, so you would have supposed that this state would be a steady progression. So it had been, for a couple of decades; but later it had become a steady retrogression. Benton was much less progressive than it had been ten years before—but somehow this didn't bother people, didn't make them feel less progressive, didn't do anything to them. Is an institution always a man's shadow shortened in the sun, the lowest common denominator of everybody in it? Benton was: the soldiers, as always, were better than the army in which they served, the superficial consenting nexus of their lives that was Benton. The people of Benton, like the rest of us, were born, fell in love, married and died, lay sleepless all night, saw the first star of evening and wished upon it, won lotteries and wept for joy. But not at Benton.

—From Randall Jarrell, *Pictures from an Institution.*

ADVERTISING

By STEPHEN WHITE

THE USES OF ADVERSITY

One of the more prominent manufacturers of cigars has seen fit, during the last few months, to establish a sort of association of his product with cowboys and Indians. This has taken place primarily in television commercials and reflects Madison Avenue's usual cultural lag; I presume the whole thing was planned when westerns were riding at their highest and then took a year and a half to whip into shape. (Remember when Scrabble was appearing in one out of six television commercials, after it had been forgotten everywhere else?) But to get back to the cigars, the entire rationale of the campaign escapes me. The average cigar smoker is scarcely likely to associate himself with either a cowboy or an Indian and would not be inclined to lay much weight on a testimonial from either. He is a city man, and to be told, as these commercials tell him, that a Phillies Cheroot is no bigger around than his trigger finger can only make him uneasy: he doesn't think of himself as possessing a trigger finger, and wouldn't know what to do with it if he had one. Finally, no cigar smoker can also be an outdoor man, since it is impossible to light a cigar alfresco, and not even very satisfactory to smoke one there. Cowboys, although rather stupid on the whole, knew this and smoked hand-rolled cigarettes that were mostly paper and hence highly inflammable.

But it is not the manifest improbability of the campaign that stimulates me so much as the fact that the cigar companies and their agencies have not yet yielded to the temptation of getting a little cut-and-slash into their advertising. "Smoke El Ropo," they might be telling the world, "and stand a reasonable chance of surviving to play with your grandchildren." Or, more succinctly, they might say, "If you must smoke, try a cigar."

Deep down, I admire their delicacy. I am aware that most cigar companies make cigarettes as well and take pains to let their left hands know what their right hands are doing. Still, there are independents, and to my knowledge they have so far discreetly laid off, which is more than Postum used to do for the coffee people.

As for the cigarette manufacturers, they must by now be well aware that they are selling products which in all likelihood are highly noxious. If they were cranberries, they would be illegal. The task set their advertisers is unique: they must allay the fear of lung cancer without ever quite admitting that it exists, for once they concede that the disease may be a consequence of the habit, they might just as well shut up shop. So they speak of "improved filters" and porous paper and that vital quarter of an inch, or they tamper with the flavor of the weed in a somewhat simple-minded attempt to imply that if it tastes like a Life Saver, it can't be very harmful.

For my own part, I have accumulated a new respect for the Camel people, who are at least logical. "Smoke a *real* cigarette," they adjure me. There is no nonsense about Camels; they are the same unabashed coffin nails they always have been. This has the merit of consistency: if you believe the medical profession, you shouldn't smoke cigarettes at all, and if you doubt the doctors, why monkey with the shape or size or contents of the cigarette? In other words, the Camel folks simply ask me to make up my own mind, and that's fair enough. At least that is the way things stand now, although if sales slip badly, I shouldn't be surprised to see Camels add clam-juice flavoring and a steel-wool filter.

I call it a unique problem, but it does have areas of resemblance to the problems faced by the liquor industry. Alcoholic beverages, after all, were once legally declared deleterious and were restored to the shelves only after it turned out that the legislation was even more deleterious. But distillers have remained very careful of how they advertise. They never suggest that Old Hotpoint will add to your geniality or make you feel good or contribute in any way to your well-being—they can't even be depended upon to make it very clear that you are supposed to drink it. A visitor from Mars, with no information other than that supplied by the liquor advertisements, could be excused for not quite knowing what one was supposed to do with the stuff—beyond standing in front of a fireplace with it. The only positive advertising placed by the Trade may be seen annually during the few days before New Year's Eve, when they urge their clientele to drink coffee.

But the advertising fraternity thrives on problems, and a catastrophe such as that which has struck the cigarette industry only serves to stimulate the copy writer's supply of adrenalin and reinforce the account executive's conviction that he is a sort of midtown Tensing Norkay, low on oxygen but always prepared to scale another peak. And at this writing, the ad men are way ahead: cigarettes are selling better than ever.

ART BY ACCIDENT

CONTINUED FROM PAGE 32

to understand this movement in order to see what, if anything, these painters and musicians are trying to tell us. In so doing we will need to relate it to the art of the past, discovering, if we can, whether the changes taking place are mere modifications of earlier tradition or are truly revolutionary. Finally, we may speculate about the validity of the aims and aesthetics of the movement.

Consider the comments thus far made. They have not been about the works of art themselves but only about the manner in which they were created. This raises a ticklish question of aesthetics. How relevant is the artist's intention in the evaluation of works of art? Clearly, sincerity alone does not make a work good. Some of the worst artists and composers who ever lived were unquestionably dedicated, serious, and sincere. On the other hand, does insincerity or accidental creation make a work of art less beautiful? Does either make it less a work of art? The question has been raised many times. One famous instance occurs in James Joyce's *Portrait of the Artist as a Young Man,* when Stephen puts the following question to his friend Lynch: "If a man hacking in fury at a block of wood . . . make there an image of a cow, is that image a work of art? If not, why not?"

For most of us, certainly, creation implies purposeful activity. The most scathing thing that one can say about a work of art is to cast doubt upon the purposefulness of its creation. To call a painting or a piece of music ugly or unpleasant is to criticize—and others may disagree. But to say "my little brother could have painted that" or "it sounded like the cat walking on the keys of the piano" is to make a remark intended to damn the work beyond hope of salvation. For what these statements really assert is that no real intention to communicate was involved in the creative act. Or to turn matters the other way around: Of what use are accounts, such as one often finds in program notes for concerts, of the "life and hard times" of the composer? They don't really help us to follow the music as it unfolds. But they may help the audience to believe in the composer's integrity and sincere intentions.

All this adds up to an important observation: namely, that we who are imbued with the values of Western thought and culture have learned to think teleologically. We have learned to believe that there is a purpose in things. Life is a directed activity focused toward envisaged goals. And implicit in the concepts of "focus" and "envisaging" is the concept of time. We live in a shifting present from which we look forward to an imagined future that we try to control by planning and prediction. Our world is one of purposeful causation and sequentially ordered time. It is the world of Aristotle's four causes, and of his beginning, middle, and end. It is also the Judaeo-Christian world with the Beginning and its Cause in the Book of Genesis and the End—the Last Judgment—and its Cause in the Revelation of Saint John.

Kinetic focus—that is, purposeful motion toward a goal—has been a salient characteristic of Western art. Think for a moment of Leonardo's *Last Supper.* The powerful lines of perspective created by the architectural organization of the room, the generally symmetrical arrangement of the figures, the relationships of the colors, all lead to a single goal: the central figure of Christ, which is itself outlined in bold relief by the lighter colors of the window behind it. Or consider the way in which the symmetrical groupings and balanced color relationships in many late Gothic paintings focus attention upon a central figure. Or how the strong directional lines in Picasso's *Guernica* literally point our passage through the painting.

Even such paintings as Bruegel's *Wedding Dance* or Van Gogh's *Starry Night,* which have no single point of attention, are developed around climactic points of interest, whose interaction organizes the painting as a whole. Moreover, though less obviously focused, such paintings create a strong sense of structured motion and, consequently, of time. The eye does not see them in a random, haphazard way but follows a path laid down for it by the artist.

Even in a generally symmetrical painting, the arrangement of spatial events cannot be reversed. For instance, if a slide of, say, Cézanne's *Still Life with Apples* is turned backward in the projector, the structural relationships of the work are almost totally destroyed. The painting "falls apart." Even though they are literally static, paintings such as these have a beginning, a middle, and an end.

Music, too—particularly since the Renaissance—has been a focused, goal-directed art. Harmony, melody, and rhythm all combine to create expectations as to the sequence of musical events and the direction of musical motion. Think, for instance, of the development section of a Beethoven symphony, moving with increasing intensity toward the focal point, the recapitulation, which will re-establish the stability of probable harmonic progression, clearly structured melodic shapes, and regular rhythmic patterns. Or consider the mounting tension of the surging sequences in the climax of Isolde's *Liebestod.* This is music of causally related events in chronological time. To change the order of parts in such a piece—to begin with the development of a sonata movement and then play the exposition and recapitulation—is as unthinkable as to play it backward.

Let us return now to that art and music in which chance is the controlling principle and consider not how it was created but what its salient characteristics are.

Meyer Shapiro, writing in *The Listener,* has observed that "a painting by Pollock . . . can be continued indefinitely without loss of character." And this seems to have been confirmed by Pollock himself, who was quoted as saying: "My paintings do not have a center . . . but depend upon the same amount of interest throughout." A similar attitude has been expressed by Stockhausen, who speaks of "creating in each piece an individual self-contained world, like a crystal which, when one turns it, is always different but always the same. It should not matter whether the music is played from the beginning, middle, or end, so long as it goes full circle. A different way of listening is required—not the analytic integrative way appropriate to classical music but one more contemplative, perhaps quasi-mystical."

Not only do the works of these artists tend to lack focus but, appropriately enough, the act of creation is itself not focused toward a goal. No vision of the end product is involved in the act of making a work of art. To use their own phrase once again: paintings aren't painted—a phrase which implies purposeful activity—they simply "happen," a word whose root significantly includes the notion of luck. "What happens on the canvas," says the painter William Baziotes, "is unpredictable and surprising to me. . . . As I work or when the painting is finished, the subject matter reveals itself."

A brief comment is in order here. Igor Stravinsky has noted that, to some extent, all artists discover the meaning and significance of their own ideas in the act of creation. Thus Shakespeare may have learned what Hamlet was really like in the very act of giving him particular words, phrases, and speeches and in having him perform certain actions. Beethoven, likewise, may have learned the real nature of his themes by discovering their inner potential as he developed them in the course of composition. But these discoveries took place within a conceptual framework that controlled the organization of the work as a whole. It was therefore different *in kind* from the methods of creation used by Stockhausen or Cage, Pollock or Mathieu.

The fact that this new "art-by-accident" is neither kinetic nor goal-oriented has consequence for the time dimension of art and music. For if there is no direction and focus, if the order of events is either absolutely arbitrary or wholly random, then time becomes mere duration. We experience time only in relation to ordered pattern change; where pattern and change are accidental, time is meaningless.

Since they are timeless and unfocused, these works are purely objective, that is, simply *there*; they do not represent anything but themselves. Hence they make no attempt to organize and shape our responses. As Peter Selz, a critic not much taken with abstract expressionism, has put it: "The finished work will often remain below the level of interpretation and distillation, so that the artist leaves us with no memorable forms or experiences. . . . The artist here presents the experience undigested and leaves it up to the viewer to do the rest."

The new aesthetic has been admirably summarized by Mathieu: "The new painting is an overthrow of Aristotle. Painting no longer has a beginning, middle, and end. It represents a timeless universe in which past, present, and future are one. There is no teleology, no direction to the universe. There is only existence—being. There is no purpose in things, they just *are*. One aims at a state of rest."

We have already had occasion to touch upon the interest which many of these artists and musicians have shown in Oriental philosophy. In part, no doubt, this interest arises from an attraction and kinship felt for Oriental art—in particular for calligraphy. According to Hubert Crehan, "Mathieu reveals his enchantment with the forms of those sacred Oriental abstract styles that were cultivated by the Zen monks of Japan. . . ." And it is worth noting that Mark Tobey, a patron saint of the movement, studied calligraphy in the Orient. Possibly John Cage, at least in his compositions for prepared piano, has been influenced by the rather precise, dry sounds of some of the music of the Far East.

More important, however, is the fact that Zen Buddhism —at least as set forth by its Western proponents—is a philosophy that perfectly expresses the moral attitude and aesthetic outlook of many of today's most advanced painters and composers.*

"Teleology," writes D. T. Suzuki, one of the important spokesmen for Zen Buddhism in the West, "is a term belonging to the world of time, relativity, causality, morality, and so on, while Zen lives beyond all these limitations." The universe is purposeless, nondirected. Alan Watts has pointed out that for Zen "the world is seen as an inseparably interrelated field or continuum, no part of which can actually be separated from the rest or valued above or below the rest." Since by a goal we mean the valuation of some things above others, then in this system goals are impossible.

Earlier Zen masters liked to illustrate the pointlessness of everyday notions of purpose and causality by answering the inquiries of their students with apparently irrational *non sequiturs*. For example, a monk asked the famous master Joshu, "When the body crumbles all to pieces and returns to dust, there eternally abides one thing. Of this I have been told, but where does this one thing abide?" To which the master replied, "It is windy again this morning." Here the validity of goals is denied not by precept but by example.

Observe, too, that in such a world accident is a legitimate —indeed the only sensible—way of making decisions. For if everything is valued equally, then there is no rational basis for choice. So you might as well flip a coin and have done.

Complementing this tenet of Zen is the belief that man is essentially good (again the opposite of the Judaeo-Christian-Freudian attitude of the West). This being the case, no justification, no purpose, no striving is necessary. For instance, one cannot *try* to achieve *satori*, a state of revelation and enlightenment. As one Zen master has said, "Externally keep yourself away from all relationships, and, internally, have no pantings [or hankerings, *ch'uan*] in your heart. . . ." Each man should be what he is, be so spontaneously, and accept the world for what it is. One should let life happen, just as one now lets paintings happen.

*See "The Square Roots of Zen" by Nancy Wilson Ross, in Horizon for July, 1959.

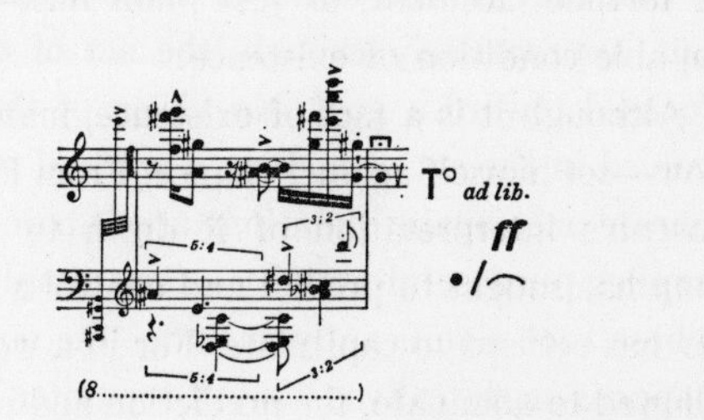

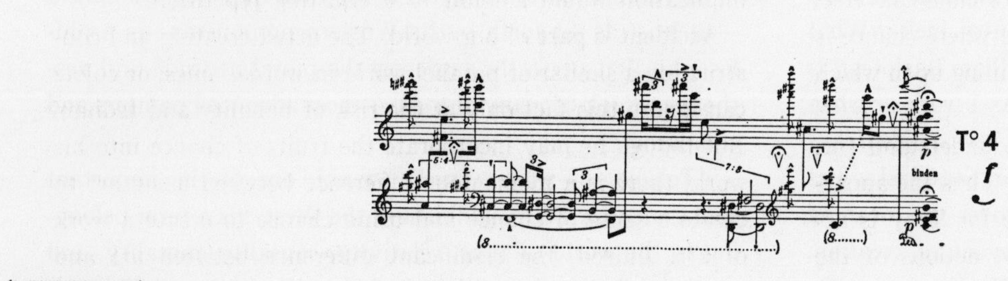

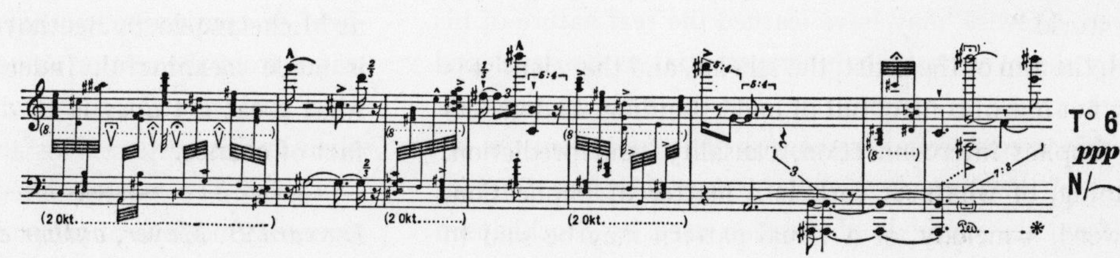

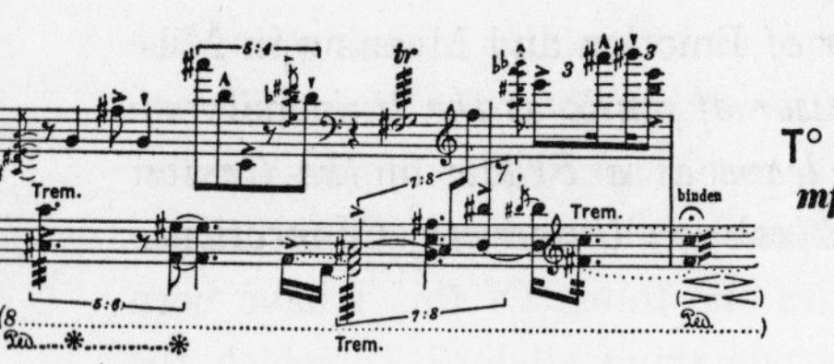

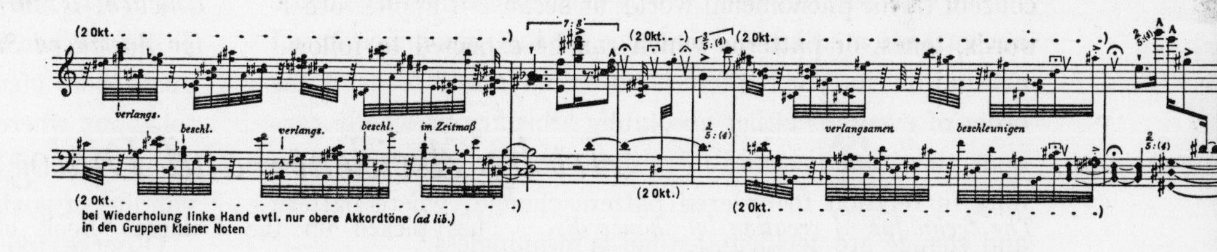

A player may begin anywhere in Stockhausen's Nr. 7 Klavierstück XI *(a portion of which is shown here), playing the fragments at random. Markings at the end of each fragment give instructions about the tempo, loudness, and attack of the next one.*

It should be clear at this point that these new directions represent not the eccentric behavior of a few publicity seekers but the work of a group of serious and thoughtful people who are creating an art which expresses a consistent, clearly defined set of attitudes and beliefs about the nature of the universe and man's place in it. It should furthermore be apparent that, though intimations of this aesthetic may perhaps be discovered in the work of earlier artists (notably that of the impressionist painters and composers), it constitutes not a minor deviation from the main current of the Western tradition but a radical revolution in attitudes and beliefs—a denial of the basic tenets of art, philosophy, science, and religion as they have been known in the West.

A pure cultural historian would probably let matters rest here, studying and analyzing the phenomenon but passing no judgment on it. And a philosophical relativist might say, "Take your pick, both are tenable positions." But the question of value—of the morality of chance as a way of creation—has already been broached. And I should like to deal with this problem, however inadequately.

Let us begin this final part of our inquiry by returning to the notion of chance. One thing is certainly clear: chance is pervasively present in the universe. A gust of wind catches a seed which, falling upon fertile ground, grows into a massive oak. A moment later its neighbor falls upon barren ground and withers. One soldier is alive and laughing, while another, standing not a foot from him, is killed by a minute fragment of a shell bursting yards away. Two sets of genes, combined by chance at a particular moment in all eternity, make each of us what he or she is. Call it what you will—fate, the wheel of fortune, accident, or just plain luck—chance is an inescapable condition of existence.

Although it is a fact of existence, man has—at least until now—set himself against chance. From Pharaoh's dream and Joseph's interpretation of it down to today's technology, man has sought to predict and control a capricious universe. He has refused to capitulate. For in a world where chance is allowed to dominate, the prediction and planning upon which survival depends would be impossible.

But control is not enough. Man needs to understand (or, if one insists, to rationalize) the accidental. Thus the apparently fortuitous ebb and flow of the battle for Troy is accounted for by the changing attitudes and actions of the Olympian gods. And three thousand years later a learned scientist, Einstein, affirming his faith, took a stand against chance. "I cannot believe," he said, "that God plays dice with the world."

Indeed, the aim of the artist, the scholar, and the scientist is primarily not one of control but of understanding. And understanding implies interconnection, causality, and prediction. For meaning, of whatever sort, is a matter of implication. Thus a word, a melody, or a visual pattern may be said to have meaning either because it refers to an object, event, or concept in the phenomenal world, or because it implies other words, tones, or patterns which can be expected to follow. Similarly, the significance of a physical, mental, or social event lies in its consequences—actual, implied, or imagined.

If the references, implication, and consequences of things are matters of mere chance (as the practice and philosophy of these artists seem to assert)—if the connections between things are not real, then the universe and existence are literally meaningless. (Of course, if one contends that the universe *is* meaningless, and life is pointless, then there is nothing more to be said. The disagreement is one of basic belief and cannot be rationally resolved.)

Nevertheless, chance exists. And for this, one should be grateful. For a totally ordered, determined, and predictable world, like a completely random world, would be both dull and meaningless: dull because it would lack tension, anticipation, and surprise; meaningless because totally determined implication would amount to everlasting repetition.

Accident is part of our world. The artist creating and constructing a similar or parallel world in words, tones, or colors can ignore this fact only at the risk of banality and tedium. But though he may incorporate the fruits of chance into his work, there is a momentous difference between using art to create a sense of chance and using chance to create a work of art. Indeed, the significant difference between art and nature lies in the fact that in art the accidental, occurring in conjunction with the probable, has implications and consequences that make it understandable. In Aeschylus as well as Michelangelo, in Beethoven as well as Shakespeare, chance is made meaningful. Indeed, one might well contend that what great art *does* is to discover significance in the brute fact of chance.

Leonard B. Meyer, author of Emotion and Meaning in Music *and an associate professor of music at the University of Chicago, is currently on leave as a Fellow of the Center for Advanced Studies at Wesleyan University, Connecticut.*

Art by Accident—and Dialogue, Too

The technique of creation by chance discussed in Mr. Meyer's article has now been applied to the drama. In June, New York's relentlessly avant-garde Living Theater Repertory produced a program of two plays under the label of "The Theater of Chance." Here is an excerpt from Walter Kerr's review in the New York Herald Tribune *of June 23, 1960:*

In "Women of Trachis" the element of Chance (fate, the hand of God, what have you) is confined to the plot; a woman creates a catastrophe she does not intend. In Jackson MacLow's curtain-raiser, "The Marrying Maiden," the element of Chance becomes the play proper, directing its dialogue, its movement, its meaning (?).

. . . We are informed that the author has picked up the Chinese "Book of Changes" and has selected, by "Chance operational systems," the words to be used in the play. Judith Malina has directed the ensuing arrangement by determining stage-business on the basis of a dice-throw or the turn of a pack of cards.

That is to say, while the characters are crawling over crossed ropes, drawing scimitars, riding on stretchers, gaping from ladders, or circling around an actor who looks like Jerry Colonna (whatever happened to Jerry Colonna? He was so funny), the material they are reciting reads something like this:

"Supreme it. Success the. Walking a slave. Dried bites in the wooden. The creative horse. Thunder. The arousing." There are filmed rehearsal-shots, only slightly inferior to the home movies I make, between scenes.

Since every work demands that it be judged by its own standards, "The Marrying Maiden" had best also be reviewed by chance. Lacking a pair of dice at the moment, I have shut my eyes and selected at random from my notes on the play—"random selectivity" is the Living Theater's phrase, not mine—the key words for this morning's estimate:

The acting at the Living Theater is mountain. Miss Malina's stage direction is extremely indeed. The musical score has a strong receptive note to it. Should you go to see it all? Inmost.

Two can play at this game.

TWILIGHT IN THE HAMMAM

Last summer I took a cruise through the Greek islands on a Greek ship, stopping at Crete and Rhodes among other places. The cruise guide was an agreeable fellow and generally accurate in the information he gave us about the classical world; but he was a patriotic Greek and, as such, woefully warped concerning one subject—the Turks. Not a word did he mention about any survival of Turkish culture in the islands: to listen to him, no one would have dreamed that the Turks, the master race in the archipelago for hundreds of years, had left any traces behind them. "Apart from its art museum, Heraklion isn't an interesting town," he told us when we were on Crete. And: "Apart from the Crusaders' architecture, there's nothing to see in the city of Rhodes."

Anyone who has done any reading about those places knows that that isn't so, of course; and fortunately I'd studied a little. I found that Heraklion had plenty of old Turkish bazaars and spent a happy afternoon wandering through them; and in a tree-shaded quarter of Rhodes, bristling with minarets, I visited half a dozen domed mosques, leaving my shoes at the door in the charge of cordial old Turks. "There are still several thousand of us living here," one of them said. "Have you visited our hammam? It's just next door. It's been functioning steadily for three hundred years." (We spoke in Italian, Italy having been the master race in charge of Rhodes from 1912 to 1945 and having left its traces superimposed on those of the Crusaders and the Turks.)

In the pages of romantic travelers, I had read entrancing descriptions of the hammams, or Turkish baths, in the Near East—lineal descendants, the writers always said, of the famous Roman baths whose vast ruins cover half the Eternal City and of which copies were constructed throughout the Empire by the Romans when *they* were the master race.* Hadn't Flaubert written to a friend from Cairo about how conducive to thought and how "very voluptuous and sweetly melancholy" it was to take a bath in one of the vast hammams there, "lost in those dark rooms under the glass dome while naked Kellaks call out to one another as they massage you, turning you over like embalmers preparing you for the tomb"? And Théophile Gautier, before finally relaxing after *his* Turkish bath in Constantinople with cups of coffee and glasses of *"limonade à la neige,"* had marveled at the delicate drops of moisture that had miraculously risen out of his own skin under the skillful hands of the Turkish masseur. It was, he said, like "the pearly dew that appears on the sides of a champagne cooler. Very unexpected."

I thought of those raptures and others like them as I entered the Rhodian hammam next to the mosque and exchanged Italian greetings with the Turkish manager. Alas! He told me at once that the place was just closing.

"But they said next door you'd been functioning steadily for three hundred years!"

"We have. But we close for three or four hours every day; that doesn't mean we let the fires go out. *They* have been burning steadily since the seventeenth century, except for once or twice during the German occupation when there wasn't any wood or coal."

We both looked somber. I knew that of all the master races in Rhodes, the Germans had stayed the shortest time but perpetrated the greatest barbarities.

Although I couldn't take a bath, he showed me his establishment—the heated marble slabs, the pool, the fountains of cool, warm, and hot water. The heat coming up through apertures in the marble turned the watery atmosphere into a vapor: there was no "steam room" per se, with jets of live steam—a true Turkish bath is a steam bath only in a very gentle sense. Just as in Flaubert's hammam in Cairo, here too there was a glass dome. But the place had about it a has-been air, rather than any feel of antiquity and glamour. The director seemed rather depressed, I thought. And finally he confided to me: "You know, Rhodes is turning into the most modern Mediterranean vacation resort. All the new hotels are full of *private bathrooms*." He almost wailed those last two words. "Modern apartments are being built here, too—with *private bathrooms.* Rhodians are installing *private bathrooms* even in their old houses. It's a disaster!"

I was glad to leave the sad little hammam. "Three hundred years, yes. But four hundred?" That seemed to be the question on the director's face as we said *arrivederci.*

In Istanbul, a couple of weeks later, I asked an American friend who lives there and works in the NATO office: "Which is the best hammam in town?"

He looked at me in surprise. "Aren't you at the Hilton? I didn't know there were any rooms there without bath."

"There aren't," I said.

(If I'd wanted to, I could have told him why I particularly enjoyed my bathroom at the Hilton. The hotel had been designed by the same New York architects who had designed my apartment house on Third Avenue, and in the bathrooms they had used the same fixtures exactly. It was amusing to find myself, in Istanbul, making precisely the same gestures, as I turned faucets on and off, that I made in New York.)

*See "Where the Romans Enjoyed 'Omnia Commoda'" in HORIZON, May, 1960.

By FRANCIS STEEGMULLER

"Then why do you want to go to a nasty old hammam?" he asked. "Put it out of your mind. Of course if you're exhausted from sightseeing or something and want a good workout, I know a Finnish couple who run an awfully good sauna just off Taksim Square. They'll scald you with steam and whip you with birch twigs and. . . ."

I thanked him coldly and changed the subject. Obviously he hadn't read Flaubert and Gautier about sweet melancholy and *limonade à la neige;* it's always tiresome to meet those anti-*fantaisie* American types while traveling.

Somehow, however, what with all my sightseeing, I kept putting off looking up an Istanbul hammam, and then one morning I took a plane to Bursa for the day. Bursa was capital of the Ottoman Empire for a while, sometime before 1453 when the Turks captured Constantinople, and it still has handsome early mosques and other ancient buildings. It's in Asia Minor, only twenty minutes by air from Istanbul.

I found Bursa to be a charming town, built on the side of a hill in beautiful rolling country. I accepted the services of a local English-speaking guide, and after he'd showed me the principal buildings, he told me that Bursa was famous for its fine water. "The town is full of hammams," he said. "Since you're a tourist, I think you ought to see the Old Hammam. It's really *quite* old. Marvelous Byzantine architecture. The Emperor Justinian had it built in the sixth century for his wife, Theodora. Theodora had bad arthritis, you know."

I hadn't known that, but I was glad to be taken to a hammam that sounded as if it might be the real old thing. And indeed the Old Hammam did turn out to be rather Flaubertian and Gautieresque. There were marble columns with fine old Byzantine capitals around the circular central pool under a dome, and all around were heated marble slabs and fountains of gushing water. But when I said to my guide: "Where do I get a towel? I want to take a bath," he was shocked. "A bath here?" he said. "But this is the *Old* Hammam. The oldest place in town. Don't you see the kind of people that bathe here?"

To me the bathers—all men—simply looked like bathers. The only thing that struck me particularly about them was their excessive modesty. Even when doing the breast stroke or the crawl in the pool they kept their towels—Turkish towels, of course—knotted around their waists. The towels kept unknotting themselves and trailing out behind the swimmers like fishtails, and whenever that happened, the swimmers would stop swimming and reknot the towels. I have seldom seen such dogged and persistent efforts at self-concealment, especially in an all-male establishment.

With bad grace my guide gave in to my whim, and we took a Turkish bath where Theodora had bathed. The other bathers—"very proletarian; very," my guide said to me—all greeted me politely and inquired through my guide how I liked their city and their hammam. I gave enthusiastic answers. Although nobody suggested a massage—so I couldn't tell whether my skin, like Gautier's, would produce a pearly, champagne-cooler dew under proper handling—still, the Bursa water made my skin feel very pleasant.

When we finished, my guide said, with the insistence of a modern-minded Turk: "You mustn't leave Bursa having seen only the oldest baths. You must see the newest, too, our wonderful establishment in the Çelik Palas Hotel."

At the Çelik Palas, men and women were swimming in a big pool that might have been any indoor hotel swimming pool anywhere; and we soon got into conversation with a blond lady in a bikini, an English-speaking Turkish housewife from Istanbul, who had certainly left the harem far behind her. She shuddered when my guide told her that I had insisted on bathing in the Old Hammam. "*This* place isn't really a hammam at all," she said. "If it were, I wouldn't be here. This is—what do you say in English?—a spa, with mineral water. Nobody's bathing here just because of the lack of a bathroom at home, like that riffraff in the Old Hammam. Everybody is here for some special reason." And we soon learned that she was bathing here because she and her husband hoped for children, and the Bursa waters were supposed to stimulate fertility. "My husband flies over from Istanbul every weekend to join me," she said. "Of course bathing isn't all we are doing in our hope for children."

I told her that I would be back in Istanbul that night and would be spending a few more days there, and asked her if there wasn't a hammam there that she could recommend to a tourist. "Where are you staying in Istanbul?" she asked.

"He's at the Hilton," my guide told her, with a giggle.

"At the Hilton!" she shrieked. "And you . . . ?" When she finished that routine she shook her head. "The only possible hammam in Istanbul is——" She told me its name, but added: "Nobody I know ever goes there any more unless they're having plumbing trouble in their apartment." And in a few words she summed up the modern-minded Turk's position: "Hammams used to be the only places to get clean in. But now we can do that in our own homes."

When I told her and my guide that there were still some well-patronized "Turkish baths" in American clubs and hotels, they laughed. "Then Turkey's ahead of America in something," the lady said.

And it turned out that there was something the lady was ahead of *me* on. I told her that I'd seen beautiful Turkish towels in the Bursa bazaars—big thick ones, with a velvety pile, in all colors: Bursa is the very home of the Turkish towel—and she put her hand on my arm. "That big thick velvety pile," she said, scornfully. "Very luxurious feeling. Yes. But does it absorb water? No. Shall I tell you where I get my bath towels?"

I nodded, and she leaned over in confidence. "I have friends in Istanbul," she said, "who have PX privileges."

Biographer, essayist, and storyteller, Francis Steegmuller is the author of The Grand Mademoiselle, *of a translation of* Madame Bovary, *and of a new novel,* The Christening Party.

FRANK LLOYD WRIGHT'S WAR ON THE FINE ARTS

CONTINUED FROM PAGE 102

Blashfield? The Puvis de Chavannes of Mrs. Potter Palmer's *Sacred Grove*? The LaFarge of the Church of the Ascension or the Frank Millet of the New York Pavilion at the Fair? In sculpture the choice would have been no wider: MacMonnies of the plaster fountains at the Fair or Karl Bitter whose *Glorification of War* was on the Administration Building (page 103), the St.-Gaudens of the *Grief*, the Hermon MacNeil of *The Sun Vow*, the Daniel Chester French of *Death Staying the Hand of the Young Sculptor*. It must be remembered that all these men and dozens more like them had been on display at the Exposition in '93. Wright would have seen them all, and we have only to look at them to understand why he had to reject them as possible collaborators.

In effect, Wright was refusing to have any commerce with either the past or the present of Western art. This was a purely negative position and one which he could not, either as designer or as ideologue, long preserve. Some alternative had to be found—and found it was, in 1893, in the Japanese exhibits at the Columbian Exposition. Here there is confusion about the exact sequence of events, much of it due to Wright himself, who could not endure the suggestion that his work was influenced by other men since "influence" was for him synonymous with "plagiarism." But we know that as Louis Sullivan's chief designer, Wright often visited Sullivan's Transportation Building when it was under construction, and he must have seen the Japanese Ho-o-den Palace and Nippon Tea House then as well as later when they were open. And he certainly saw the great show of Japanese prints, architecture, and sculpture in the Fine Arts Palace.

Whatever the details, the impact of the Japanese print upon Wright (as upon many Western artists of his generation) was catalytic, electrifying. For an architect it opened up a whole new system of aesthetics which illumined not only the formal problems of painting (composition, color, delineation, and so on) but introduced an organically unified tradition of architecture, landscape, and furniture design. He was thus attracted to the Japanese for much the same reasons as the American artists James McNeill Whistler and Lafcadio Hearn. And, considering that architecture is a much more obdurate medium than painting or poetry, his response is quite prompt. It may be a full decade before the lessons from the Japanese are fully digested, a fact announced by the stunning houses for the Willitses (1902) or the Martins (1903–04). But already in the same year as the Fair, the Winslow house shows us that the change in Wright has begun; and succeeding years show us how his whole artistic life is being irradiated by Hokusai and Hiroshige.

Here, as elsewhere, his work in actual architecture is fully paced by essays explaining his thinking. And from them we can see how profoundly he was moved by the principles of Japanese art and how little danger there ever was of his merely copying their forms. At the personal level, the Japanese print taught him the "gospel of simplification . . . that organic integrity within the work of art itself is fundamentally a law of beauty." The astringent simplicity of the Japanese deflates the mock heroics of Western art, showing that "a sand bank and the sea . . . may yield a higher message . . . than Angelo's magnificent pictorial sculpture. [The print] has taught that sentiment has nothing in common with sentimentality or sensuous feeling with sensuality."

What dazzled Wright in Japanese art was its power of abstraction, its capacity for extracting from complex and turgid reality the artistic essence of each problem. This power enabled Wright to cut his last ties, both with eclectic architectural idioms and with art forms full of raw gesture and anecdote. It taught him both what had to be done and how to do it, and the fertilizing effect is both apparent in his work and generously admitted in his essays.

But he had meanwhile drawn another, more generalized and even more significant conclusion from his experience with Japanese art. It was completely foreign to our own artistic tradition. Precisely because of this "ethnic eccentricity," as he put it, "this art is a particularly safe means of cultivation for us because the individual initiative of the artist is not paralyzed with forms he can use ready-made." This is an observation which deserves our attention, for it reveals a very clear understanding, on Wright's part, of the cultural dynamics of the period. The world of American art in 1900 was drowned in and saturated with forms from the Western past. They were umbilically tied, by history and literature, to set responses and attitudes. It was therefore impossible for the young American to study them, so to speak, clinically.

Wright does not claim for Oriental art any unique mastery of the simplified, the distilled essential, the truly abstracted. He is quite aware that these properties reside in all great art, of West and East alike. What he is arguing here is that they can be studied by the young artist and designer with more clarity and detachment in Oriental than in Western examples. Just because it is so eccentric to the orbit of his own prejudices, he can study Oriental art without crippling entanglements, with an objectivity which he simply could not bring to bear on his own artistic tradition.

It is a matter of sad record that few architects or artists, in 1906, were willing or able to follow Wright's advice. Yet as if to prove to the world that these principles *would* work, in sculpture and mural as well as in architecture, he produced the Midway Gardens in 1913. Here, in this most festive of all his projects, he made a wider and bolder use of independent art forms than he ever had before or ever would again. He was determined to solve the problem, even if it meant doing sculpture and mural with his own bare hands. "I clearly saw my trusty T square and aspiring triangle as a means to the end I had in mind." As a matter of fact, there was a young sculptor named Ianelli on the Midway job. About his exact contributions, Wright is vague, if amiable. But the great interior mural so oddly reminiscent of Kandinsky (page 103); the smaller geometric bas-reliefs in cast concrete; the lovely caryatids around the garden wall, half geisha and half Gibson girl, warm and tender for all their cubist modeling (page 103)—all these bear the indelible mark of Wright's own genius.

It was not, perhaps, great art—Wright certainly never claimed that it was—but it was peculiarly happy for its purpose. Viewed in its context, it stands up very well indeed. It was apparently Wright's last effort to establish a working relationship with the other arts. It was certainly the last building in which the explicit statement of art was to occupy a position of such importance. From then on, art, ornament, and decoration become increasingly subdued, abstracted, and oblique in statement or meaning—that is, they become "organic to the structure."

To recapitulate: there was a time when Wright was so conscious of the need to integrate the plastic arts with architecture that he deliberately sought those forms which would harmonize with his own. He did not find them; and though he might have been as strong willed and arrogant then as he was half a century later when he designed the Guggenheim Museum, it cannot be said that the fault was wholly his. For history has proved his standards to have been correct.

This failure to establish contact with the fine arts was, in later years, to congeal into a contemptuous isolation. Architecture, always the most important, was destined to become the only art. Similarly, the mistaken painters and sculptors of his youth were to become, imperceptibly with the passing years, typical of all artists. This was a tragedy, for us as much as for Wright. He proceeded to hew out for himself a beautiful, strong, and astonishingly complete aesthetic. Yet it was, at the same time, a uniquely private system. Just as there was little room for collaboration with other artists when he was alive, there is little chance of direct progeny now that he is dead.

The new museum expresses this tragic fact; yet that Wright's policy was a wise one, during that hazardous quarter century between 1887 and 1913, there can be no question. It enabled him to produce that great constellation of beautiful structures from the Larkin Building (1904), Unity Church (1906), the Coonley, Gilmore, and Robie houses (1908–09) to Taliesin I (1911) and the Midway Gardens. No other architect in America, no other architect in the whole world, could match his creativity during these golden years.

James Marston Fitch, Associate Professor of Architecture at Columbia University, is the author of American Building *and* American Gardens. *He writes often for the architectural press.*

Mr. Wright makes himself clear: a recollection

One day in 1956, when I was working as a student in the drafting room at Taliesin West, an angry voice boomed out: "To hell with the rectilinear framework of reference!" I looked up, startled, and there was Mr. Wright striding toward me past the rows of empty drafting tables. He stopped at the one next to mine, propped up an arch-shaped replica of one of the murals he had conceived for the Midway Gardens more than forty years before (similar to the one on page 103), and silently began to touch it up.

"I have just received word," he said suddenly, "from the non-objective artists that are to hang in the Guggenheim Museum." I looked up to find him smiling.

"What did they say, Mr. Wright?"

"They say they object to their paintings being exhibited in the museum because it doesn't conform to the rectilinear framework of reference. In simple language, they want a rectangular building instead of mine because their paintings are rectangular in shape. They also want the dome-skylight changed completely—more structural support in case of fire."

As soon as he said this, I knew that it was the real reason for his agitation. His original design for the dome had been a beautiful one of interconnecting circles consonant with the plan of the whole building, and so I asked: "But didn't you do the same type of dome for the Johnson Wax building?"

"Yes," he said, "the very same: hollow glass tubes supported by a circular frame. They think that by making me change the dome-skylight I might throw up my hands and quit. No—we'll change the dome for them and the museum will be built."

He stepped up to add some color to the painting. "There, it's finished."

I went over to Mr. Wright's drafting table to look at it. "It should be put over the entrance of the Guggenheim Museum," I said to him.

"Not a bad idea! Then they couldn't ignore the true origin of the new idea in art."

"Well, you see, Kandinsky, a European, is acclaimed as the foremost originator of this new idea in modern art—called non-objective art. Now, this arch painting I've just finished is *pre*-Kandinsky. I was doing these paintings in 1898, even before the twentieth century started. The origin of the new idea in modern art and architecture is *American*, not European."

"But what is the reason for doing this arch painting now?" I asked.

"I'm doing it now to objectify this pre-Kandinsky thesis. I have created an objective painting that is not rectangular in shape."

"I see," I said. "You're disproving the non-objective artists' claim that their paintings need a rectilinear frame."

"Correct. And so this arch painting is objective painting. As for *non*-objective painting—well, now at least it will be in its proper place in the Guggenheim Museum; it will have some *objective,* for once." Then he added: "Not much, I'm afraid." He picked up a pencil and began to write something in the corner of the arch painting. When he had finished, he got up and walked away. I leaned over to see what he had written. There in the corner of the painting was inscribed: "To hell with the rectilinear framework of reference —Frank Lloyd Wright." I looked toward the door and he was gone.

—DENNIS WHELAN

This old Russian cartoon of a "Glorious Glutton" may be a veiled allusion to the voracious appetites of Peter the Great

Where Nothing Succeeds Like Excess

In Russia—which has no middle ground, only extremes—a "scarlet thread" of extravagance runs through the Czarist past no less than the collectivized present

It has been said that Russia is not a state but a whole world —a whole world where everything is on another scale: where excess prevails. Extravagance is the Russians' predominant characteristic. The tempo of their everyday lives seems, to other less extravagant peoples, a compound of violence and inertia, both carried to extremes, in love or war, politics, human relationships, architecture, or anything else.

All through the literature of Russia we trace violent emotions and excessive actions. Some of Dostoevsky's characters appear almost incomprehensible to the more restrained West. Goncharov's Oblomov carried his inertia to such violent lengths that he lolled away his whole life on the sofa. In real life we see many similarly excessive gestures: Peter the Great executing an unfaithful mistress, Mrs. Hamilton—nothing remarkable here, in history's long procession of tyrannic royal lovers, but the Czar went so far as to preserve her head in spirits, a pickled *gage d'amour* which must have been singularly dampening to the ardors of the alcove.

Continuing the excessive, or emphatic vein, we find Count Besborodko, a keen whist player, causing a cannon to be fired every time his partner revoked. Another ardent gentleman, on being repeatedly put off by the lady of his choice, throughout spring and summer, with her promise to give him an answer "when the snows came," could wait no longer; and so, during one dark night, he ordered hundreds of tons of salt to be spread over the landscape surrounding his lady-love's house. Next day, he called: "Give me my answer; the snows are here." We are not surprised to learn the lady was

By LESLEY BLANCH

CULVER SERVICE

Hypnotic, mystical, and debauched, the self-styled "monk" Rasputin held the Czarina Alexandra in thrall until his excesses led to his own murder and, though indirectly, to the outbreak of the revolution in 1917.

at last won. Alexander Pushkin's family, both the purebred Russian stock and those descended from Hannibal, the Abyssinian protégé of Peter the Great, were, in all things, excessive, even going so far as to hang an erring tutor in the courtyard.

Mighty Potemkin—the lover of Catherine the Great—was the apotheosis, the embodiment, of all Russian excess, with his unappeased appetites, furious energies, limitless resolves, and inconsequent oddities. "I am God's spoiled child," he would say. Having gratified every whim, he married the Empress, established her empire, accumulated colossal fortunes, made love to a hundred women, "talked divinity to his generals and tactics to his bishops"; and, his nails bitten to the quick, he would sit, covered in magnificent diamond orders, gnawing raw turnips, his brow furrowed, thinking intently—thinking of that vast Russian empire he was building for his Catherine. Or he would sit brooding over a collection of caskets, each crammed with precious stones which he would sort, arrange, and rearrange, voluptuously though absently, as he planned some flamboyant coup.

Even on the march and at his camp, Potemkin liked to create around him the sumptuous atmosphere of the imperial palace at Tsarskoe Selo. His silken tents were adorned with gilt mirrors and malachite urns. Sometimes he was dressed with equal splendor, pomaded and perfumed, his coat glittering with diamonds, while he worked on state papers with such savage energy that he reduced relays of secretaries to fainting point. Sometimes, for days on end, he would not bother to dress; and he would even arrive at state receptions, or a ball, wrapped in a tattered (though ermine-lined) dressing gown spotted with ink and grease, a crumpled nightshirt dragging below, from which appeared his bare, hairy legs, and feet thrust into Turkish slippers. After calling for as many as fifteen (golden) beakers of cabbage soup, at intervals of a few minutes, he would roar for coffee—and when it was brought, turn away, tears welling from his one Cyclops eye. "Take it away. . . . I only wanted to long for something. You have done me out of my pleasure. . . ."

God's spoiled child was extravagant to the end. Far from his beloved Empress, death overtook him in the south, near Jassy, as he was heading homeward. He ordered his great gilded traveling coach to stop. "Lift me out. I want to die in a field," he said. "He lived on gold, but he died on grass," said his Cossacks, watching by the huge body. No golden coin could be found to close his one eye, but a copper kopeck served well enough. It was in keeping with the life of this Russian giant, which had always swung from one extreme to the other.

Excess—and its offshoot eccentricity—how it colors the somber Russian landscape! Countess Saltikov's favorite hairdresser kept in a cage, lest he should be tempted to work for anyone else; Ivan the Terrible's architect, according to legend, blinded after he had completed the church of Vasili Blazhenni: it was to be unique. Wicked landowners were known to have forced serf mothers to abandon their babies, the better to nourish litters of purebred greyhound puppies at the breast. Fabulously wealthy nobles sent their bailiffs as far afield as Dresden or Sèvres to purchase five-hundred-piece dinner services, which were then laboriously transferred by wagon to Moscow or Ryazan or any other province, where, in one splendidly extravagant debauch, after being loaded with a Gargantuan feast of suckling pig, stuffed carp, and sturgeon, they were used as targets for a shooting contest.

Count Skavronsky, an enthusiastic musician, compelled his entire household to address him, and each other, in recitative. Another nobleman never risked the ennuis of travel without being accompanied by a cow to provide fresh milk, and twenty carriages (lined with sable) loaded with actors and musicians busy rehearsing their lines and tuning their fiddles, ready for the next halt.

The Empress Elizabeth's fifteen thousand dresses show an equal extravagance, while her habit of cutting out the tongue of anyone who lied to her contradicted her absolute refusal (on humanitarian grounds) to sign a single death warrant.

Just as the great Russian houses were staffed by an excessive number of servants (Countess Orlov, with eight hundred, complained she could never get a glass of tea when she wanted one), so prodigious numbers of house guests were

TEXT CONTINUED FROM PAGE 131

north; she mistrusted Europe's resources and always traveled with a huge trunk filled with logs. Another princess, Zeneïde Wolkonsky, who had been converted to Catholicism and was adored by the Roman poor for her unbridled generosity, died as a result of her extravagant kindness. She had noticed a beggar woman shivering in a doorway, and tore off her own warm petticoats to protect her. She herself went home sneezing and died of exposure, extravagant even in death.

"Fu una principessa russa," said the poor of Rome as they followed her coffin, wailing. They could not foresee that it was to be a dirge for all her kind—that legion of flamboyant Russian nobles who have now vanished forever. If they still linger on, more modestly, they have learned that what passed for the spectacular and the picturesque when they were rich is merely regarded as ridiculous or undisciplined now that they are poor.

Among the classic, nineteenth-century Russian idealists and political dreamers, men like Alexander Herzen, Bakunin, and Ogarev, the scarlet thread of excess showed itself strong and clear against the somber texture of their existence. Whole lives were dissipated in conversation, in interminable political discussions, in needless journeys undertaken on the spur of the moment—such as one cited by Herzen: its object, vaguely formed, "to see what was going on in the Caucasus."

The scene is London, a house at Paddington Green, where Alexander Bakunin was then living. Although he had become a revolutionary of world fame, he continued the pattern of life much as he had lived it when a student in Moscow. Here is Herzen describing Bakunin's *ambiance*:

"He used to receive anyone, at all times, everywhere. Often he would be asleep . . . or tossing on his bed, which creaked under him, while two or three Slavs would be in his bedroom, smoking with desperate haste; he would get up, souse himself with water, and at the same moment, proceed to instruct them . . . telling them they must try to find Garibaldi, to be received by Mazzini, to reach Kossuth. . . . He was not too much given to weighing every circumstance, looking only toward the ultimate goal, and took the second month of pregnancy for the ninth. He carried us away, not by his arguments, but by his hopes."

In the middle of all his arguments, lectures, arrangements, and shouted orders, this leonine figure would rush to his writing table, ". . . clear a little space among the cigarette ash, and begin to write a number of letters, to Semipalatinsk, or Arad, Belgrade, Constantinople, or Bessarabia. . . . His activity, his laziness, his appetite, his titanic stature, and the everlasting perspiration he was in, everything about him was on a superhuman scale"—was, in fact, excessive.

Herzen goes on to describe the arrival of a young Russian

COLLECTION VIOLLET

The Empress Elizabeth Petrovna (Peter the Great's daughter) considered herself the most beautiful woman in the world, changed her clothes six times a day, and once had a lady of the court whipped (and the end of her tongue cut off) for imprudently wearing pink—a color reserved for the Empress.

SOVFOTO

forever arriving, but seldom leaving. Time and distance were differently computed in Russia; yet, in a sense, they were interdependent. If, to visit friends, it was necessary to travel a thousand or more miles by carriage or sleigh, people were apt to pack up and move in for a whole season. Time seemed as measureless as the land. Some visitors came for a summer and stayed for ten years. Some lived in a remote wing of the house and, we are told, never found their way to the dining room or met their host, but just settled down among other guests: poor relations, tutors, *dames de compagnie,* and French governesses whose stay had outlived their usefulness. There they remained, embalmed in this universe of emptiness, the vacuum of their days occasionally broken by the sound of carriage wheels or bells: a sudden stir of life, telling of the arrival or departure of the family that had forgotten their existence or—carrying even vagueness to excess—had never remarked their presence.

The Russian army, too, reflected this quality of excess. During the reign of Paul I (perhaps the most extreme of all the Russians), men were marched off the parade ground and headed north, in chains, for the matter of a missing button. The officers took to stuffing their pockets with all their available bank notes; thus, if victimized without warning, they would at least have some ready cash to aid them in their exile. Even in their attitude of blind devotion to the Crown, the Russian military caste showed excess. We read of that guardsman who, as late as the beginning of this century, was walking along the Nevsky Prospekt in St. Petersburg and encountered a band of drunken agitators who spat on him. Having returned to the barracks and finished his duties for the day, he blew out his brains, leaving a letter stating that since the Czar's uniform had been dishonored by rabble spittle while *he* was wearing it, no other course was open to him. And everyone agreed it was a worthy end.

Russian grand dukes could usually be relied on to behave with the most spectacular excess, gambling at Baden-Baden or dueling in the Bois de Boulogne over some celebrated *poule de luxe.* Occasionally a grand duke persuaded some such lady to visit his Russian estates. She was as much a sensation in Russia as he had been in Paris, appearing at bear hunts in *toilettes* from the Rue de la Paix, distracting the beaters as well as the guns. She would return home decked with splendid jewels and telling stories of sleighs festooned with emeralds, or snows strewn with Parma violets rushed from Grasse to prove the ducal lover had not forgotten his inamorata's favorite flower.

During the nineteenth century, Rome had plenty of opportunities to observe the extravagant Slav nature. Many of the wealthy Russian émigrés gravitated there, centering round the Wolkonsky family, who are still commemorated by the Villa and Via Wolkonsky. Princess Sophie dreaded a timber shortage, a lack of firewood, after leaving her vast Russian estates where an infinity of forests stretched to the

TEXT CONTINUED ON PAGE 134

In 1580, Ivan the Terrible got into a fight with his eldest son. It started as a silly family quarrel—over an "immodest" gown the Czar's daughter-in-law was wearing—but it grew so violent that Ivan, in a blind rage, struck his son on the head with a steel-tipped staff. The blow was fatal. Ivan wept, tore his hair, sent alms to the churches, and threatened to abdicate (but didn't). This picture of the grief-maddened Czar with his son's body is a detail from a painting by I. E. Repin, which is now hanging in the Tretyakov Gallery in Moscow. OVERLEAF: *Two more examples of Russian flamboyance—a monster "fountain" of gymnasts performing at a Soviet Sports Day demonstration, and the domes of Saint Basil's Cathedral on Moscow's Red Square.*

officer burning for the Cause—for Liberty—who had succeeded in escaping from Russia, and whose goal was to meet Bakunin. He had only arrived the night before, but a friend undertook to bring them together.

" 'I'm sure you won't refuse to do something for the common cause,' says Bakunin.

" 'Of course not,' replies the young officer.

" 'There is nothing that detains you here?'

" 'Nothing; I have only just arrived, I . . .'

" 'Then, can you take this letter to Jassy, at once? From there you must make your way to the Caucasus. We particularly need a trustworthy man there.' "

The extravagant Slav temperament was to be traced in all classes of society and was never more marked than in the whole nation's positively abandoned attitude toward suffering. *Toska,* a sort of inner misery, a neuralgia of the soul, a compound of *cafard* and spleen, permeated the nineteenth-century Russian nature (and is, even now, the hallmark of the émigré and not yet entirely subdued by the collective living, calisthenics, and Five-Year Plans of the contemporary USSR). *Dousha,* the soul—ever a matter for introspective discussion among the classic Russians, as portrayed in their literature—was generally held to represent the *suffering* soul. This occupied a special place, becoming a national attribute, almost a matter of pride—like sex to the French.

Russian peasants, in particular, were partial to songs which dwelt on their sufferings—not of the body, as might have been expected, but of the soul. This was born of their hopeless condition. For the middle classes, it derived from the stultification of their lives, while satiety and egotism bred it even stronger in the aristocracy. There was a whole tradition of these suffering songs beloved by the villagers (and still sung by collective-farm workers), their shrill harmonies accompanied by balalaika and accordion, echoing over the rolling wheat fields and steppes, heard at dusk across the sunflower plantations of the Ukraine, along the sandy flats of the great rivers—Tikhii Don . . . Quiet Don, and Mother Volga.

Grisha! thy soul suffers for me! Go! Suffer for another.
My soul suffers for Vadim,
My tears are shed for him.

They were lusty in their grief, savoring it to the full.

Even the wealthy merchants and privileged nobility subscribed to this cult and enjoyed nothing more than to spend whole nights of expensively fostered misery, listening to the gypsy choirs who knew that for every wild drinking chorus, every bacchanal, their audiences really craved some melancholic soul-song. The gypsies sat on benches round the walls of some stark private room of a restaurant or inn, the men shaggy and sullen, the women bunched in shawls and buttoned into uninteresting dresses, many of them the most unprepossessing-looking matrons. They stared straight before them, their black, untamed stare piercing the haze of smoke

When Catherine the Great made her royal progresses, Potemkin would patch up the most miserable villages and put a few well-dressed peasants on view in order to deceive her about the state of Russian prosperity.

and the fumes of vodka, singing their haunting airs while their listeners became maddened and intoxicated by misery, transported by the obsessive quality of singers and songs, of sadness and suffering souls alike. Whereas in England the old wives' panacea has ever been "a good cry," the Slavs went further and were apt to nationalize their grief. Dostoevsky's Lizaveta Prokofyevna points to Myshkin, saying: "I've had a real *Russian* cry over him."

The suffering soul was not confined within the frontiers of Russia alone; the nineteenth-century Russians took it with them into political exile, along with their samovars and icons, and were to be seen sitting in cafés, discussing the state of their souls as earnestly as any constructive program. They were a strange blend of despair and optimism, grandiose schemes, futility, and petty bickerings. As the century progressed, anarchists and terrorists superseded the first idealists, but even *they* sometimes stopped experimenting with a new bomb formula to luxuriate in discussions about the miseries of the soul. Man cannot live by bombs alone.

Today, the Russian peoples, while retaining a certain Oriental fatalism, have learned to replace futility by purpose and to sublimate the emotions which ravaged Herzen and his circle. These earlier idealists irradiated the last glow of purely personal sufferings. Party took the place of person, and Communism was formed. Seething emotionalism was canalized into one collective whole, where action, Five-Year Plans, and superhuman efforts had the effect of occupational therapy and overcame the last faint echoes of *toska*.

Yet excess remains: it is the core of the Russian peoples, their strength and weakness, at once their comic relief (to the outside observer) and their glory. It is the key to both their past and their present, and it must mold their future too. It is often incomprehensible to the West, puzzling and frightening, like the force of nature which, at heart, it is. Anyone who has known and lived among the Russian peoples, anyone who is steeped in their literature or studies their history, becomes aware of this quality, or elemental force—excess. Thus we see, in the history of Russia, that it sweeps on its way, like the symbolic troika of which Gogol wrote, thundering forward, once centuries behind the West, but suddenly outpacing the rest of the world in its furious forward dash, over and across every obstacle, over lives and ideologies, but ever onward toward its own goal. As Madame de Staël observed, "The imagination of the Russians knows no limits; with them everything is colossal rather than well proportioned, impetuous rather than well considered, and if they do not attain their goal, it is because they have gone beyond it."

Lesley Blanch's study of Russian excess will appear in her newest book, The Sabres of Paradise*—an account of the 19th-century Murid Wars in the Caucasus. She earlier wrote* The Wilder Shores of Love, *and is the wife of novelist Romain Gary, until recently French Consul General in Los Angeles.*

SOVFOTO

When a 17th-century Turkish sultan threatened the Zaporog Cossacks, they replied with typical Russian violence by composing a letter calling him, among other things—and this is the mildest—"son of a dog." Repin's painting re-creates the scene.